Ethics
A Beginner's Guide

"Rich, comprehensive and provocative, with illustrative examples that are original and stimulating... altogether a fine and authoritative introduction to the subject."

Michael Clark – Emeritus Professor of Philosophy,
University of Nottingham

"A must-read. It is thorough and complete, yet always accessible and entertaining, written in Cave's signature sharp style. No matter what your background, this book will inform and challenge you – just as moral philosophizing should."

Andrew Pessin – Professor of Philosophy,
Connecticut College

"Readable and entertaining... With characteristic verve, Peter Cave surveys a wide range of topics and challenges readers to think their way through complex moral problems. For those seeking to make sense of life's dilemmas, as well as for students enrolled in philosophy courses, this is an ideal guide."

Dan Cohn-Sherbok – Professor Emeritus of Judaism,
University of Wales

ONEWORLD BEGINNER'S GUIDES combine an original, inventive, and engaging approach with expert analysis on subjects ranging from art and history to religion and politics, and everything in-between. Innovative and affordable, books in the series are perfect for anyone curious about the way the world works and the big ideas of our time.

Ethics
A Beginner's Guide

Peter Cave

ONEWORLD

A Oneworld Paperback Original

Published in North America, Great Britain and Australia by
Oneworld Publications, 2015

ISBN 978-1-78074-576-3
eISBN 978-1-78074-577-0

Typeset by Tetragon, London
Printed and bound in Great Britain by Clays Ltd, St Ives plc

Oneworld Publications
10 Bloomsbury Street
London WC1B 3SR
England

Written for
those who anguish about
doing what is right –
and for those who do not

♈

In memory of
Laurence Goldstein (1947–2014),
good friend, good philosopher,
good humoured –
and now, sadly,
goodbye

Contents

SOME ETHICS

Tzu Kung asked, 'Is there any single saying that one can act upon all day and every day?'

The master said, 'Never do to others what you would not like them to do to you.'

Confucius (*c.* 551–479 BC)

The unexamined life is not worth living.

Socrates (*c.* 469–399 BC)

For what shall it profit a man, if he shall gaine the whole world, and lose his owne soule?

Jesus (*c.* 5 BC–27 AD)

That Action is best, which procures the greatest Happiness for the greatest numbers; and that, worst, which, in like manner, occasions Misery.

Francis Hutcheson (1694–1746)

Two things fill me with wonder: the starry sky above and the moral law within.

Immanuel Kant (1724–1804)

If we possess our why of life we can put up with almost any how. – Man does not strive after happiness; only the Englishman does that.

Friedrich Nietzsche (1844–1900)

Our duty can be defined as that action which will cause more good to exist in the universe than any possible alternative.

G. E. Moore (1873–1958)

Grub first; then ethics.

Bertolt Brecht (1898–1956)

A man without ethics is a wild beast loosed upon this world.

Albert Camus (1913–60)

Prologue:
the moral medley

Noel Coward, so the story goes, sent postcards to a selection of distinguished establishment people. The cards said, 'We know what you've done. Leave London or all will be revealed.' They all left London – well, so it is reported. Nothing was revealed – save, later, the facts here presented.

Whether or not the report is true, most of us – if not all – recognize that we have done things we ought not to have done, or failed to do things we ought to have done. Those 'ought's could be read in terms of securing our own advantage. Many, though, recognize that such 'ought's and 'ought not's possess moral flavours, not those of any obvious self-interest. Perhaps we let someone down or betrayed a confidence; broke a promise or were not quite honest about payments received; or passed by on the other side. We readily recognize how we may be ashamed of certain behaviours – certain hopes, motives and emotions – and yet proud of others. Such reflections place us in the realm of ethics, of morality; such reflections show our ready awareness of morality, of ethics – and hence of this book's subject.

Ethics, as an academic discipline, is, of course, the study of ethics, of morality; it is a reflection whereby we self-conscious beings seek to make sense of how to live. In our everyday lives, we often wonder what we ought morally to do. That can lead into questions of what would be fair or just – yet also, whether one should be loyal or impartial, courageous, compassionate… Would it be beneficial overall to lie on a particular occasion? Is it sometimes better not to insist on our 'rights'? And so on... The 'and so on' leads into the nature of goodness, of moral responsibility, and into life and death dilemmas – abortion, sexuality, assisted dying, our treatment of non-human animals. Ethics embraces a medley of moral concepts, concerns and questions.

The terms 'ethics' and 'morality' are typically used interchangeably – as they are here, until Chapter Ten – though 'ethics' perhaps hints at the ethos of a life whereas 'morality' focuses more on duties and rights. For completeness, let us mention political philosophy: although its central concern can be procedures for effective government, underlying must be the moral justification of a state's authority and how it prioritizes moral values such as liberty, welfare and the democratic will. European states, for example, reject capital punishment, the death penalty, considering it morally repulsive, whereas some US states have no qualms at all in applying that penalty of finality.

Ethical study sometimes focuses on particular businesses, professions or cultures; professionals – nurses, teachers, journalists – refer to their professional ethics. A profession carries special duties, duties of care that apply to their charges, but not thereby to outsiders. Individuals may also speak of their own ethics by which they endeavour to live, ashamed when they fall below the standards set. Ethics, as a discipline, would then be studying the ethos advanced.

Banks, for example, promote codes of ethics, codes which merit analysis and evaluation. We may reflect – sadly reflect – how bad things have come to pass when such institutions need to declare explicitly that they treat customers fairly and with honesty. We may worry about their true intentions, just as suspicions arise when individuals repeat, 'Trust me'. Codes of ethics can be but marketing masks to help generate greater profits, enhanced power or increased membership and recognition; witness financial institutions' free portfolio reviews, manufacturers' 'improved' products quietly designed with built-in obsolescence, and fun cartoon downloads for children – all devised to stimulate sales.

♈

This book confines itself to ethical approaches currently examined in Western philosophy. Although current, they are grounded in ideas discussed by philosophers for over two thousand years, ideas manifested in everyday lives across the world – East and West, North and South. After an introductory chapter, six chapters review the major positions, including stances sceptical of the whole moral enterprise. The outcome, it is hoped, is greater awareness of the medley of concerns – all correctly understood as *moral* – yet concerns that, in the author's view, inevitably conflict and lack common measure; they are a muddle. Of course, the selection and weight given to objections and replies are the author's, the aim being to stimulate readers into further reading and reflections. The last three chapters and Epilogue explore the medley's relevance to practical matters, from the human to the ecological, returning finally to the fundamental ethical concern of how to live. Inevitably in that finality, the author's stamp, a somewhat melancholic stamp, is there to see – for readers to take to task and show where mistaken, or for readers to explore and enhance, based on their own experiences and reflections.

Philosophy, it has been said, is thinking in slow motion. With ethical problems there are temptations to blurt out quick answers, as if something is obviously right or clearly wrong. We need to think slowly, reflect and imagine possibilities; we need to take our time. Humility can be a virtue. It certainly is where philosophical thinking is concerned and when trying to see morality aright – and hence what is morally right.

WHAT DOES MORALITY DEMAND?

The Tram: A driverless tram is hurtling towards five workers trapped on the rails. They will all be killed, unless... You are at the points; you could divert the tram onto a siding, where only one worker is trapped. If you divert, one person is killed. If you do nothing, five are killed. You could walk on by, keeping your hands clean – or would they be so easily cleansed? What *ought* you to do?

Here is a revision. The only way you can stop the tram – saving the five – is by throwing a bulky man onto the track. He will be killed, but the five will be saved. Ought you to throw?

The Bear: Two friends are hiking through woods when they become aware of a hungry bear heading their way, eager to eat. 'We'd better run for it,' says one. 'What's the point?' sighs the other, 'We can't outrun a bear.' 'No need to do that,' is the smug reply, 'I just need to outrun you.'

Morally it would surely be wrong for one deliberately to trip up the other; but is it morally permitted for one to 'save her own skin', leaving the friend to fend for herself?

The Violinist: After minor medical procedures, you awake to find a violinist attached to you via a tube. You learn he was in urgent need of cells that only your blood can supply. If you unplug, he dies. The tubing is inconvenient: wherever you go, the violinist goes too. He pleads with you not to unplug.

Are you within your rights to unplug, although it leads to his death? Even if within your rights, is it morally permissible for you to unplug? May the answer rest upon the duration he must remain plugged and the length of tubing? Maybe the hospital often does involuntary pluggings; if so, did you know?

Extending the tubing, so to speak: reflect on how, as consumers, we are plugged into others, their lives and environments, thousands of miles away, affecting those others and being ourselves affected.

1

How ought we to live?

How ought we to live? That is the central question of ethics and arguably the most important question in life – well, perhaps the second most important, second to the question of whether we should continue to live at all. That question of suicide was for Albert Camus 'the one truly serious philosophical problem'.

'How *ought* we to live?' We probably all face that concern at some time or other, whether explicitly or not. It was raised by Socrates in the fifth century BC as the fundamental question, not just for ethics, but for philosophy as a whole. It was, said Socrates, a question everyone should ask; it is not confined to philosophers, the intelligent or educated. How ought *I* to live? Perhaps correct answers differ depending upon who we are; perhaps the question arises even if I am the sole person, the sole creature on the planet.

'When I'm good, I'm very, very good; when I'm bad, I'm better'

Ethics is concerned with the good – and much more – but as Mae West's quip above may suggest, terms such as 'good' and 'bad' can confuse, even amuse. We may wonder what is needed for 'the good life'. Does a good life require us to be morally good? Is moral goodness enough for us to live a good life? Perhaps it invariably needs supplementation by, for example, wine, roses and chocolate – even philosophy.

Putting to one side ambiguities of 'good' and related terms – the varieties of goodness – we confront a medley of moral concepts, from vices to virtues, from wrongs to rights, and of moral questions raised by, for example, vast wealth inequalities, freedom of expression and military interventions on humanitarian grounds. Let us mention a few other examples.

Many people across the world are in desperate need of clean water, food and medical facilities; the better-off make occasional charitable donations, but could easily give more, relinquishing a few luxuries. Ought not they – ought not we – to be far more generous and benevolent? Some people believe sexual promiscuity immoral; others keenly embrace that promiscuity, yet judge sex for money as immoral. Is that not inconsistent? Under the slogan 'bad things happen to good people', the US Pasadena Police Authority permits prison-cell upgrades for a fee, an opportunity unfair and of no use to prison inmates at the bottom of the ladder. Is not the policy morally repugnant, with the Authority lacking either sensitivity or concern for justice? Is that policy so very different, though, from those of many jurisdictions? Frequently, punishments are monetary fines which the rich guilty can pay, probably affecting their lives not at all, while the poor, unable to pay, can end up in prison.

Moral problems and conflicts stir some to propound slogans such as: ethics is a matter of choice; morality is relative, relative to your society – or police authority. Others justify morality through religion: God tells us what is right and wrong, with the sinful being those who neglect God's commands. Religions sometimes speak of evils – evils understood as satanic, malevolent forces that go beyond the simple badness of failing to do what is right.

Moral codes exist in the ancient religions of Hinduism, Zoroastrianism and Judaism. Codes were prescribed by Confucius (c. 551–479 BC) and Buddha (c. 450 BC), though not with any typical divine base. With Jesus (*c.* 5 BC–27 AD) and Muhammad (570–632), we again encounter morality grounded in divine presence. Later, in Catholicism, Christian morality became mingled with pre-Christian Greek thought, for example, with Aristotelian philosophy by way of the writings of St Thomas Aquinas, a major thirteenth-century philosopher.

The Socratic question of how to live is hence often answered in terms of moral laws, laws that must be followed because divine or because aiding harmonious living. Recently, some have turned to science, aiming to justify moral awareness as needed for human survival, essential to evolutionary self-interest.

Whom do you admire?

With competing approaches to morality, we may feel at sea; so, let us find some dry land. Consider the following:

> A man takes his vicious hound into the park; he deliberately sets the beast onto a mother and child. They are badly mauled; the man laughs. That man has acted wrongly. That judgement is an understatement. He has behaved appallingly.

> A woman, dressed in her finery, hurries to an important interview. On her way, she sees a man collapse, his mouth frothing blood. She dashes to his assistance, puts her cashmere coat under his blood-seeping head, calls an ambulance, reassures him, waits with him. She has surely done the right thing; she has behaved with tenderness and fellow-feeling.

Our cameos could say more about the participants and circumstances. One thing upon which we no doubt agree is that the hound owner behaved badly; the woman behaved well. It would be troubling, to say the least, if readers doubted that. We accept the principle that, in such circumstances, it is wrong to set hounds onto people.

In saying an action is right or wrong, we are guiding or encouraging behaviour; that seems all we are doing, hence 'right' and 'wrong' are sometimes termed *thin* concepts. Weightier concepts – *thick* concepts – are also morally relevant. The man's behaviour was despicable and atrocious. The woman was kind, compassionate, admirable. Such value-laden terms frequently occur in our discourse, without particular moral reflections. Think of references to discourtesies, brashness, timidity; to composure, dignity, 'going the extra mile' – where we describe behaviour or characteristics, while also expressing attitudes for or against.

There are numerous cases where we all (more or less), without theories in mind, agree whether an action merits ethical approval – or the opposite. That risks sounding as if ethical matters should be decided by majority votes, opinion polls or laboratory investigations uncovering people's assessments of right and wrong in various imaginary cases. That is a mistake. Morality is no matter of majority opinion. There can be a right and wrong about right and wrong. Majorities sometimes get things wrong. Many people in some societies – sometimes a majority – have believed enforced slavery morally acceptable, the Earth flat and that human sacrifices appease the gods. We fall into error about the physical world; we also err about the ethical.

The hound owner gains pleasure from hurting others, but that is no good way to live, given the effect on the others. Further, such pleasures may not constitute a good way of living *for him*. Can the hound owner truly be respecting himself? Contrast the woman who helped the collapsed individual. She may have lost a job because she missed the interview, yet would not – in a sense, *could not* – have respected herself had she walked on by.

Numerous clear-cut cases of immoral and moral behaviour could be given; but there are also numerous moral dilemmas. Some argue that, in principle, there is always a definitive right answer to such dilemmas; others reply – the author is one – that that is not so.

> A father is close to death. He is worried about his daughter, working for a charity in war-torn lands. You know she is having a dreadful time, but you deceive him, reassuring him all is well. Is that the right thing to do?
>
> We feel morally uneasy at buying inexpensive clothing and foods – inexpensive because they are produced in distant lands by child labour, 'bonded labour', a modern version of slavery. If we do not buy, families in those distant lands may well be made even worse off. What ought we to do?
>
> From afar, you witness a gang beating up a teenager and then running off. You could identify the ringleaders to the police, but you fear the consequences for your son and yourself. Ought you to put your family at risk?

The dilemmas remind us of the very different circumstances in which ethical questions arise. Fortunately for many of us, there are few or no occasions when we face dilemmas that require heroism, or where we are likely to collapse into spectacular wickedness. As a further point, there is a danger of seeing morality as solely arising when conscious choices are being made about what we should do; we need, though, to have a sense of how a life unfolds, often without our noticing – for good or ill.

Egoism: why do we do what we do?

Some scorn morality. They argue that we always act for our own sake, in our own self-interest or, more accurately, in what we perceive to be self-interest. Such psychological egoism differs from egotism, the excessive use of 'I' and similar. A different egoism, ethical egoism, is that we *ought* always to act self-interestedly. Egoisms do not automatically dismiss concern for others; they do not have to legitimize thugs who get power, wealth and sex – and get away with it. Ethical egoists may argue about what is *truly* in one's self-interest, and that may be, for example, contemplation or purity of the soul; such a highly moralized gloss to self-interest can be found in Socrates and Plato. Here, we consider the more typical understanding of 'self-interest'.

Is it our natural state always to act without any genuine concern for others? Evidence counts against it. Although we witness much self-interest, we also spy actions where self-interest appears far from the motive.

You do not want to visit your aged aunt – it is a nuisance – but she likes your company, so you make the effort to please her, and not because of possible inheritances. 'Ah,' is the reply, 'you visit her for inner glows in which to wallow; other people will praise you for doing the right thing.' Yet, even if you inwardly glow, the expected glow or praise may not have been your motivation. Sometimes people act simply for the sake of others. Parents help children for the children's sake. Environmentalists save the beached whale for the sake of that whale beached.

Adam Smith, the eighteenth-century Scottish economist, is often cited as valuing self-interest. Self-interested actions of the wealthy, via the 'invisible hand' of the markets, advance the interests of society. 'It is not from the benevolence of the butcher, the brewer, or the baker, that we expect our dinner, but from their regard to their own interest.' Smith, though, also recognized that:

> How selfish soever man may be supposed, there are evidently some principles in his nature, which interest him in the fortune of others, and render their happiness necessary to him, though he derives nothing from it except the pleasure of seeing it.

DO WE ALWAYS ACT IN OUR OWN SELF-INTEREST?

Thomas Hobbes (1588–1679), a highly influential political philosopher, seemed to hold that we always act from perceived self-interest. His view was not quite so crude, but John Aubrey noted:

> **Hobbes was very charitable** (to the best of his ability) to those that were true objects of his bounty. One time, I remember, going in the Strand, a poor and infirmed old man craved his alms. He, beholding him with eyes of pity and compassion, put his hand in his pocket, and gave him 6 pence. Said a divine (Dr Jaspar Mayne): 'Would you have done this, if it had not been Christ's command?' 'Yea,' said he. 'Why?' quoth the other. 'Because I was in pain to consider the miserable condition of the old man; and now my alms, giving him some relief, doth also ease me.'

Bishop Joseph Butler (1692–1752) mocked Hobbes's evidence for universal self-interest, for our always seeking our ease:

> **Suppose a man of learning** writing a grave book upon Human Nature... and the following would need to be accounted for: the appearance of benevolence and good-will in men in natural relation, and in other relations. Cautious of being deceived with outward show, he retires within himself to see exactly, what is in the mind of man from whence this appearance proceeds; and upon deep reflection, asserts the principle to be only the love of power, and delight in its exercise.

Self-interest was Hobbes's motivation, but that reflected badly on Hobbes, says Butler, not on mankind: we do not always act in our perceived self-interest; and it is not rational always so to do.

Saving a theory

Look around: we see people helping others for the sake of the others – true, not often enough. Only if we already hold a theory denying altruism's possibility, would we insist that such selfless acts are 'really' self-interested. For deniers, nothing is allowed to count against the theory that all actions are self-interested; 'selfless' actions have been defined out of existence – but that does not change the reality.

Egoists may insist that Smith's comment still highlights self-interest: the interests of others are pursued purely for the pleasures of self – as Aubrey reported of Hobbes (please see insert, p. 7).

Observations of selfless acts perhaps fail to convince the sceptical because their belief in universal self-interest is closed to empirical counter-evidence, to the possibility of falsification. Hobbes, for example, insisted that 'the object of voluntary acts is some good to himself' the agent; yes, there is love, good will and charity, but they provide people with the delight in their own power. Anything we do must be because of something internal to us; at some level, we want to do it, hoping to reap satisfactions. We even perform moral duties to satisfy our desire to perform those duties; so those performances must also be self-interested.

A curious switch in the meaning of words has occurred in the above reasoning. Suppose we fall in line with that switch, agreeing that everything we do necessarily is from self-interest: we should then need to distinguish between people who, from self-interest, want to do things for the sake of others, and those who, from self-interest, do not. By way of quip, we should still need to distinguish between those who do things for free and those who do things only for a fee.

In dismissing self-interest as the way in which we do always live, we have not, of course, explained how we *ought to* live – whether there can be a justified morality that trumps ethical egoists' claims that we ought to act self-interestedly. It is worth noting here that there can be reasons why people should act in certain ways, even though they do not recognize them. A girl is about to fall off the swing; you run to save her. Perhaps your wanting to save her explains your action; but, whether or not you want to help, whether or not you go to help, averting the tragedy is still a reason why you should. Whether it is a reason that outweighs, say, your reason for rushing on by is, of course, another question.

Before we examine some highly influential moral theories

that seek to draw us away from simple self-interest, we need some fundamental distinctions, to avoid subsequent confusions.

Good and bad moves: orientations

Within a game of chess there are good and bad moves, but that has no standing with regard to the nature of the morally good and bad. Further, it says nothing about whether chess-playing is itself a good or bad activity. Laetitia may be good at tennis, a bad public speaker and someone who knows the right way to smuggle a man into college. Those are not – well, are not usually – accolades or condemnations of an ethical nature, but descriptions of how well or badly she performs things, just as a knife may be excellent for cutting and a poacher bad at poaching. The good way to commit murders without being caught involves leaving no self-incriminating evidence; but that does not present murder and evasion of detection as good. We place such uses dependent on functions to one side, though we shall see later that Aristotle modelled the good man as one excellent in functioning as a rational animal – which, sceptics may quip, rules out relevance to vast numbers of us.

There is a major distinction – the 'is/ought' distinction – between describing and prescribing, between saying what *is* the case – the factual – contrasting with what *ought* to be the case, the normative. Care is needed: when saying that something is right or wrong, we are on the 'ought' and 'ought not' – the normative – side of the distinction. Further, 'ought' is not always the 'ought' of morality. That you ought to wear the turquoise earrings may concern fashion; but that you ought to obey the law is likely to be a moral demand, though it could be some non-moral guidance for avoidance of fines. When Machiavelli enjoined political leaders to do what they ought to retain power, even if necessitating murder, he may have been making an amoral technical point, not addressing the morality of means or end. It could be deemed immoral, though, even to discuss certain matters, such as murder, in amoral terms, as if murder's immorality is open to debate.

Morality differs from legality. Legally it is permissible to protect your property from someone desperate for shelter – to own second homes usually left empty, while others are homeless – yet we may doubt the morality. Something that is legal is not thereby morally acceptable. Further, something that is illegal may yet be the right thing to do; for example, opposing immoral laws that oppress racial minorities or an impoverished majority. The legal and the moral can overlap: both morality and law usually maintain that killing innocents is wrong.

When evaluating an individual's – a company's, a nation's – morality, we may be searching for underlying principles, their consistency and consequences of adherence. Some individuals insist that the taking of life is morally wrong: we may ask, then, why they kill animals for dinner, execute murderers and do nothing to prevent people elsewhere from dying? They may have excellent answers, revealing that their principle needs caveats – or they may change their behaviour and stick with the principle. Of course, some simply do not care, content to live with hypocrisy and inconsistency.

Another evaluation aims directly at the moral principles themselves. Here confusion can arise. A people may promote a particular morality, with no contradiction between its principles, yet the 'morality' is immoral. One morality may judge another – may morally judge another. That is readily seen when confronted by people with a religious-based morality. Witness how one religion often condemns another as containing immoralities. Within a single religion, condemnations can arise: some Christians understand homosexual relations as morally corrupt; others do not.

When philosophers seek to establish which actions are right, which are wrong, which states are good, which are bad, they are engaged in 'normative ethics', determining norms or values by which we should live. Normative theories provide a platform for applied ethics, for the application of theory to practical situations – for example, those of redistributive taxation, factory farming and wars in which civilians will be harmed. Can morality be shown to permit or even demand such activities? We could become nuanced, distinguishing between the normative (telling us our duties) and the evaluative. We may evaluate some people as good people without thinking it our duty, or the norm, to imitate them; we may praise those devoted to saving the whale, yet not think it our duty to maintain such devotion.

Normative ethics is a splendid discipline, but philosophers sometimes retreat from providing moral instruction books or enjoining moral sensitivities. Stepping back, they focus on the nature of moral talk, on meta-ethics (sometimes known as 'analytic ethics'). There is the semantic meta-ethical task of establishing the meaning of terms such as 'good' and 'bad', leading to metaphysical questions of whether objects possess moral properties 'out there' and, if so, the epistemological or 'knowledge' question arises of how we gain acquaintance of those properties. The distinction between the normative and the meta-ethical is not as sharp as some suggest. In the next chapter, the normative theory of utilitarianism may be telling us what we really mean when we speak of the morally right and the morally wrong.

♈

Time to step into theory – and how theory touches the practice of everyday living. Let us, then, give way to the utilitarians – to see the colours in which they paint morality and the extent, if any, to which their concerns strike moral chords. Whether the metaphor is colour or sound, utilitarianism sets off with the tremendous appeal of happiness. Now, what can go wrong with that?

ETHICS FROM THE ANCIENT GREEKS

How should we live? 'Well and happy', is the typical answer of Greek philosophers. That sounds self-interested, conflicting with morality's regard for others. Greek philosophers thought otherwise.

Socrates (469–399 BC): The truly virtuous person cannot be harmed. That is the astonishing Socratic view. Socrates identifies the person not with the body, but with the soul. To live well is to possess the goods of the soul, the virtues: courage, justice, piety, wisdom. They form a unity. Being essentially of the soul, not the body, a person's goodness is immune to material misfortunes.

Plato (428–347 BC): As with Socrates, the self is the non-physical soul – now seen as tripartite, with a spirited part, a pleasure-seeking part and reason. The soul flourishes when reason rules, bringing inner harmony or justice – as the flourishing city is one that is just, with its citizens in harmony. Philosophical reasoning aims at acquaintance with Goodness, an abstract Form transcending individual human lives, which may yet inspire us in its perfection.

Aristotle (384–322 BC): The soul is the form of the body, a distinctive functioning of the human organism. Hence, worldly elements come into play for the good life, the happy life (see Chapter Four). The virtues are personal excellences of human character; they do not guarantee a flourishing life, but they increase its likelihood.

Epicurus (341–270 BC): For Epicureans, pleasure is the sole good. We must learn how to live without anxiety and pain. Living well requires risk avoidance. We should value simple pleasures, friendships, refraining from harmful activities and superstitions about gods and afterlives. Being dead is to be nothing; it is nothing to be feared.

Stoicism (founder Zeno of Citrium 344–262 BC): Happiness is living in accord with nature, our rational nature. Marcus Aurelius argued that distresses arise from judging events as damaging, when we need not. Rational control, right judgement, can free us from enslavement to lusts, envy and greed, guarding us from misfortunes. Stoics sought tranquillity – and were much mocked by Nietzsche (see p. 97).

2

Utilitarianism: maximizing happiness

'You ought to maximize happiness.' That is the heart of ethics according to utilitarianism. The theory is highly influential, if only by way of stimulating many philosophers and those of religious faith to react with disdain. 'Surely, human beings are no lowly animals, no mere seekers after pleasures, after happiness.' Others run to the theory's defence, providing a utilitarian justification; after all, asks Jeremy Bentham, what ultimate appeal other than to happiness could ever sensibly be made? If it is wrong to lie, it is because lies typically lead to unhappiness; if wrong to torture, that is because of the sufferings. When lying seems to be right – when torturing is defended – justifications involve avoidance of greater suffering. 'If you tell the truth, it will break him.' 'If you fail to extract the information, thousands will be maimed.' When torture is condemned outright, the appeal again is to overall happiness; torture is ineffective or brutalizes us, reducing happiness in the long run.

The greatest happiness of the greatest number

This section's title, from Bentham, locates the utilitarian heart. In John Stuart Mill's words:

> The creed which accepts as the foundation of morals, Utility, or the Greatest Happiness Principle, holds that actions are right in proportion as they tend to promote happiness, wrong as they tend to produce the reverse of happiness.

Utilitarianism is consequentialist (as the term is used today) – the most influential consequentialist moral theory. It is teleological, assessing actions by outcome, the end, the *telos*. The actions themselves may be pleasurable, so those pleasures enter the calculations. The theory, by definition, is hedonistic, its key value being happiness. Sometimes the stress is on maximizing welfare; sometimes minimizing suffering. Most people recognize suffering, pain, as a great bad, far worse in its disvalue than the intrinsic positive value of pleasure; we feel urgent needs to prevent suffering, but not so urgent to create pleasure. The Greatest Happiness Principle sums up what has become known as '*act* utilitarianism'. The 'act' qualification is omitted here, until variant utilitarianisms – indirect utilitarianisms – are to the fore.

Utilitarianism is a cognitivist moral position: 'cognitivist' because, in judging actions right, we are judging matters of fact, apparently cognizant, knowing, of truths. Good states of affairs are those of happiness; right actions secure the good. The *good*, the consequential good – in this case, happiness – is prior to the *right*. Some philosophers distinguish sharply between the right and the good, though the terms are often used more or less synonymously: actions that are right may equally well be deemed good. The idea, though, is that right actions are obligatory – what we morally ought to do – whereas the good is what is morally desirable or worthwhile. The right, so to speak, commands us; the good attracts us. For utilitarians, right actions, to be right, must be for the good, that is, for the greatest happiness.

The term 'utility' is sometimes understood to mean whatever leads to happiness, and sometimes happiness itself. 'Utility' possesses an austere functional ring, so let us speak of happiness.

Bentham's happiness is solely a matter of pleasure and absence of pain. One immediate worry is that some people gain pleasure from inflicting pain on non-consenting others; why consider those pleasures valuable? Perhaps such pleasures can lack utilitarian support because of reduced overall happiness; but perhaps there is something intrinsically bad, not resting upon consequences, about pleasure in others' suffering. Another worry is that, paradoxically, utilitarian reasoning could lead to *not* helping others: suppose we provide dinners and temporary comfort, at festival times, for some down-and-outs. They are pleased. On returning to hungry sleeping on streets, though, they suffer all the more, now aware of how much better things could be for them; perhaps they now, understandably, experience painful feelings of resentment at the lucky wealthy.

Utilitarians seek to include all pleasures and all pains in their 'felicific calculus'. Happiness is to be quantified by units of pleasure, pains being units of negative pleasure. The units – mythical or theoretical entities – have been labelled 'hedons'. Actions lead to so many hedons, the quantity depending on intensity of pleasures, of pains, duration, fecundity (in leading to more) and likelihood. Quantity is key, not the source or nature of actions leading to the pleasures. Here is Bentham:

> Prejudice apart, the game of push-pin is of equal value with the arts and sciences of music and poetry. If the game of push-pin furnish more pleasure, it is more valuable than either.

Many would welcome Bentham's view: any pop song's lyrics are as valuable as Shakespeare's sonnets, if generating the same quantities of hedons. Musicals could well be more valuable than Britten's operas and rap music more than Schubert's lieder – for mass culture generates more pleasure, given larger numbers pleasured. Maybe aesthetic value is being conflated here with moral value; but even were Bentham to recognize greater aesthetic value

BENTHAM: DEALING IN LIGHT INSTEAD OF DARKNESS

Jeremy Bentham (1748–1832) founded modern-day utilitarianism. Although others tied morality to greatest happiness – Francis Hutcheson; Joseph Priestley, discoverer of oxygen – Bentham developed the theory and promoted it, passing the flame to John Stuart Mill.

Bentham was reading a bulky English history at age three, and soon after, learning Latin. He became a great social reformer, sceptical of religion, viewing it a juggernaut – The Jug – produced by superstition and ancestor-worship, as was the English common law. Reason should lead to the alleviation of suffering. With that in mind, he designed a 'frigidarium', an ice-house, for perishable foods, and a prison 'panopticon', enabling wardens to control prisoner activity from a central panoramic view.

Pain and pleasure: Nature, wrote Bentham, has placed us under two sovereign masters, pain and pleasure, determining what we do and what we ought to do. Hence, the law should be grounded in codes to maximize pleasures, minimize pains, not in abstract concepts of inalienable human rights or natural rights granted by God – 'nonsense on stilts'. He proposed ministries for health, education and reduction of indigence (poverty); he supported universal suffrage and secret ballots.

Although frustrated in love, he argued that sexual relations were typically beneficial because of the pleasures; so, he advocated legalized prostitution and, for the times, courageously proposed the legalization of homosexual acts – let people scratch where it itches.

The 'auto-icon': Bentham – well, his skeleton, his so-called auto-icon dressed in his clothes – can be found in the cloisters of University College London. He was (so to speak) spiritual founder of that first University of London, the first British university without religious tests, creating 'the godless students of Gower Street'.

Based on human desire for overall pleasure, reason and law were to rear 'the fabric of felicity' – for, insisted Bentham:

> Systems which attempt to question that... deal in sounds instead of sense, in caprice instead of reason, in darkness instead of light.

in Poussin's paintings than Peter Cave's drawings, which artistic endeavours ought to be displayed hangs on resultant pleasure. The Cave drawings may generate more overall pleasure through laughter at his masterly incompetence.

Some, particularly economists, speak of maximizing satisfactions – of desires, of preferences. Caution is required. Even when certain desires are satisfied, we may be far from satisfied overall. Witness King Midas: he seemed to secure what he desired – for everything he touched turned to gold – yet, when his touch turned his daughter to gold, he realized the folly of his desire. Further, the powerful, be they corporate, governmental or religious, can manipulate our desires. We adapt to circumstances rather than to what is best for us: for example, the enslaved, knowing nothing better, can be frightened of being set free. Further still, if desire satisfaction is all that is valuable, then, to use Plato's example, why not sprinkle ourselves with itching powder, leading to intense scratching satisfactions?

Bentham's simple, uniform understanding of pleasure was challenged by Mill. Mill had noted how many people reacted with inveterate dislike of Bentham's pleasure.

> To suppose that life has (as they express it) no higher end than pleasure – no better and nobler object of desire – they designate as utterly mean and grovelling; as a doctrine worthy only of swine, to whom the followers of Epicurus were contemptuously likened…

Mill's response was that of the Epicureans: the accusation supposed humans to be capable solely of swinish pleasures – but that supposition is mistaken. Mill continued:

> Socrates would rather choose to be Socrates dissatisfied than a pig satisfied. The pig probably would not, but then the pig knows only one side of the question: Socrates knows both.

Mill, believing qualitative differences exist between pleasures, would have valued Schubert's lieder as providing higher pleasures than rap music. Mill would have lacked sympathy for the observation of Samuel Butler, *Erewhon*'s author, who wrote:

> I should like to like Schumann's music better than I do; I dare say I could make myself like it better if I tried; but I do not like having to try to make myself like things; I like things that make me like them at once and no try at all.

Returning to Schubert, had Mill known, he would have condemned Schubert's smoking, drinking and sexual cavortings – Schubert's 'slough of moral degradation' – for Mill spoke of the absurdly disproportionate time mankind occupied itself with lower pleasures such as sex. Higher pleasures, for example, poetry, are more valuable than lower, such as push-pin. There are, of course, difficulties in determining the higher; further, with no common measure for pleasures, the utilitarian ideal of a hedonistic calculation is much weakened, if not made impossible.

Let us reflect a little more on pleasure. Pleasurable experiences are valuable, but often, so too are their sources, the objects of the experiences, and our sharing them with others. The most pleasurable activities, paradoxically, are not pleasurable solely because of the pleasure. Were the pleasure all that mattered, then we should be as pleased with a drug injection that gave us the pleasures resulting from a lover's kiss or attending an operatic performance as with engaging in the real thing.

Let us reflect a little more on happiness. Happiness involving contentment is valuable, but happiness also requires struggles, painful struggles, perhaps to develop worthwhile talents or achieve desirable ends – even to solve crossword puzzles. Many pleasures, once over, strike us as worthless in contrast to accomplishments that retain value. Even when deceased, it remains true that, for example, Harold was a fine craftsman or maintained his dignity despite reversals in fortune. An enriched understanding of happiness as a fulfilled life – we meet that concept, *eudaimonia*, in Chapter Four – involves more than pleasure; it can involve reputation and accomplishments, for they remain even after one's last breath. Mill, indeed, understood happiness as including nobility, appreciation of music and the love of virtue for its own sake. That understanding raises problems, given Mill's overarching utilitarianism; it is certainly a far cry from Bentham's concept of happiness as open to calculation.

What makes a theory a moral theory?

Utilitarianism possesses two features often deemed essential to moral theory: universality and impartiality. Examining those features will help our appreciation of the look of typical moral theories as well as leading us into distinctive utilitarian problems.

Talk of 'theory' is of a moral principle or set of principles that has something comprehensive to say about how we ought to act. We should not think much of a moral theory if all it delivers is the restricted injunction not to tread on toes or steal hats. A theory, as well as containing comprehensive principles from which particular injunctions (such as the prohibition on toe-treading) derive, highlights certain concepts as fundamental. Utilitarianism highlights consequences for overall happiness; other theories highlight rights, natural goods or virtuous dispositions.

Utilitarianism commits morality to universality: its morality applies to everyone. A principle could, though, possess universal application, yet be highly partial: the universal principle could be that we should all (including the elderly) ignore the interests of the elderly. Utilitarianism, though, claims impartiality: well, to the extent that pleasures count equally, if of equal intensity and duration, irrespective of whether the individuals pleasured are lords or serfs, old or young, European or Asian – or, for that matter, human beings, pigeons, or philosophers. It is thus a cosmopolitan theory.

The feature not ignored is happiness. Universality and impartiality align with the common sense appeal, 'Put yourselves in their shoes'.

Universality and impartiality are not sufficient for a theory to be a moral theory. That no one can travel faster than light is universal and applies impartially, but is not in the moral arena. Morality's universality and impartiality sets the framework for how we ought to act, not how we do or cannot help but act. The framework's content is, of course, also highly morally relevant. A universal and impartial theory could be that we ought to torture as many people as we can, irrespective of colour and creed. That injunction is not recognizable as part of a moral theory, though people could advocate such (immoral) living. Some, far less radically, insist that everyone ought always to act in his own interests. That egoist recommendation – apparently Ayn Rand, the US-based novelist, held that position – would, superficially at least, conflict with morality's concern for others; it would need careful argument in support. For example, acting out of (enlightened) self-interest could perhaps be the most likely means to secure overall happiness, or it may be argued that self-interest is intrinsically tied up with the moral virtues (to be seen in Chapter 4).

Utilitarianism raises another typical worry: morality's foundations. What is the source of the Greatest Happiness Principle? Has it been plucked from the heavens? Is it blindingly obvious? Or is there some reasoning to demonstrate its truth? That introduces the connection between theory and common intuitions, our common sense. Any moral theory must have initial regard for what we take, pre-theoretically, as morally evident. If, from a moral theory, the conclusion is that we ought now to kill men without beards, we should rightly think that something has gone wrong with the theory. How, then, does the basic utilitarian idea survive, when considering particular intuitions?

You are walking along a winding road on a mountain's edge; behind you, the road has been crumbling. A coach is approaching, packed with passengers. You could let it carry on its merry way to a fatal and un-merry ending – or you could hail it down, saving many lives. Surely, morality demands that you do the latter. You ought not to think, 'Nothing to do with me', or, if a journalist, 'Let's wait to photograph the disaster'.

Similar pre-theoretic cases suggest that what underlies our moral certainties is the utilitarian principle that we ought to maximize happiness, welfare, or at least minimize suffering.

Some people ask you the time of the train. You could lie, causing them to miss the train, their holiday plans ruined. True, you may secure a small amount of *schadenfreude*, of dubious personal happiness; but the right action is surely to tell the truth.

Again, this harmonizes with utilitarianism: telling the truth here is likely to maximize overall happiness. Perhaps, though – as we shall see later – the rightness of truth-telling has nothing to do with happiness.

We could muddy waters. The train-seekers are in fact terrorists in disguise, planning to bomb the train, causing numerous casualties. If we know that, morally we ought not to be helping them. That reasoning, though, also aims at maximizing happiness, hence providing more nourishment for utilitarians. On the surface, the theory has a lot going for it.

Utilitarianism looks to the future, the dim and distant as well as the near. Opponents eagerly stress how distant futures are unknown. Who knows whether saving a young woman, in the coach scenario above, will mean that later on she will bear children, leading, generations later, to the birth of a Hitler-like figure who causes millions to suffer? Utilitarians – as we all do every day – have to rely on what it is reasonable to believe about future possibilities. Without further evidence, we have to be neutral regarding distant unknown consequences of saving lives now.

A moral theory, as seen with utilitarianism, may accord with certain basic moral beliefs. The theory, with such support, can then determine what morally ought to be done in different circumstances – and that may challenge other commonsensical beliefs. For example, if the Greatest Happiness Principle attracts us, then if we must choose between saving only one life and saving many lives, we should undoubtedly take the many-saving option (assuming lives with equal happiness potential). In the runaway tram example (p. xv), where five workers will be killed unless an intervention is made, we ought to divert the tram, even though someone else, a lone man on the siding, will be killed as a result. That is good, basic utilitarian reasoning, yet many people baulk at 'playing God' in such a way.

Suppose utilitarianism leads us to accept that the tram diversion is morally required, even though probably psychologically challenging. Now suppose the only way of stopping the tram – and hence saving the five (or even five hundred and five) lives – is by pushing a reluctant bulky man, an innocent passer-by, off a bridge, in front of the oncoming tram, halting the tram and killing the man. There would be five (or five hundred and five) people saved, one person killed, as previously. Many feel, however, that we ought not to push, even though we ought to divert. Now suppose those moral intuitions are right – divert in the first scenario, not push in the second – what explains or justifies that difference?

One justification, derived from Immanuel Kant, forthcoming in Chapter Three, is that people ought not to be used solely as means to an end. The bulky man is being used – to save the others. In the diversion case, if the solo man on the track escaped being hit by the diverted tram, the five would still be saved. The solo man's death is foreseen, but neither his presence nor his death is necessary for the saving; neither advances the aim of saving the five. The bulky man's tram-stopping presence is required, even if not theoretically his death; perhaps his stopping the tram 'magically' leaves him alive, but he has still been used just as a means to a desirable end.

As those examples illustrate, moral theories respect certain basic moral intuitions, yet can lead to revision of others; but which intuitions should be taken as most self-evident? Moral theories are not justifying our basic moral intuitions; rather certain of those intuitions stimulate us into proposing the theory. We have to start from particular cases. A fundamental starting point for some, though, may be no starting point at all for others. In some societies, human sacrifice to appease the gods has been taken as a basic given; in others, moral norms include infanticide, honour killings or suttee (where a widow sacrifices herself on her husband's funeral pyre). Such differences lead to wild claims that all morality is relative. Those claims are to be rejected (please see 'The folly of relativism', p. 108). Starting with particular cases is not peculiar to ethics and the humanities. In 'hard' logic, we start with particular arguments – 'All men are mortal; Socrates is a man; therefore Socrates is mortal' – which we see as obviously valid. From such instances, we formulate rules of logic.

That in the end – and in the beginning – we turn to particular examples to assess moral principles may lead to 'particularism'. Particularists doubt the value of principles; why not stay with the particulars? Looking at where principles lead is, though, a useful way of seeing how we would handle examples, real and imaginary. Principles that charm non-particularists can highlight considerations that may aid us when reflecting on what ought to be done in particular cases; still further reflection may then show how those principles fail to accommodate moral complexities, the principles thus requiring caveats or rejection.

How is happiness to be distributed?

There are many cases, as we have seen, where utilitarian reasoning accords with moral intuitions. The following is an example that most would accept.

You are a surgeon; you can either have your usual rest day or work additional hours to operate on some surprise emergency casualties. Unless more factors enter the tale, for utilitarians you ought to forgo the rest day and perform the operations. Your loss of pleasure given the extra work is swamped by the victims' pleasures in having, say, their limbs saved.

There are, though, many cases where, but for fancy footwork, utilitarianism clashes with common sense morality: for example, the tram tale's second scenario. Although common sense should not always have the last word, we should surely not use an innocent passer-by as a heavy brake, even to save many others. Utilitarianism does not merely permit such seeming immoralities; it demands them – even demanding that the bulky man offer himself up (or down) as sacrificial saviour.

Until nuances arrive, killing a healthy person, for example, to save five lives by distribution of his organs, is a utilitarian requirement; after all, letting the five die has the same consequential outcome as killing the five. Consequentialists see no intrinsic distinction, morally relevant, between 'acts and omissions'. Further, doing nothing, foreseeing the death of the five, is, on the surface, morally equivalent to intending their death. If consequences are the key, then the alleged moral distinction between intending and foreseeing, as promoted in the Doctrine of Double Effect (please see p. 58), lacks moral significance – unless some consequential differences flow.

Returning to the surgeon scenario, probably greater overall happiness would be secured if the surgeon sacrificed all his luxuries – unnecessary rest days, family life – and spent his wakeful, skilful time in operating theatres. Many of us, certainly the author and many readers, could reduce living standards to help the dispossessed, the starving and the ill. Although our happiness would diminish, the reduced suffering of others could more than compensate for our loss of some happiness.

Utilitarian morality demands far more than most of us can stomach. Utilitarianism, it seems, commits the morally minded to become, so to speak, saints. It allows no room for 'going beyond duty' – for supererogation – because there is nothing beyond duty. To overcome that objection, the requirement to maximize happiness is sometimes replaced by that of doing enough (satisficing utilitarianism) or at least of increasing overall happiness by some degree (progressive utilitarianism).

Note how our common sense intuitions are generating changes to the theory; those particular proposed changes suffer from obvious difficulties in judging and justifying the 'enough'.

We are engaging puzzles of the just, of the moral distribution of goods. For utilitarians, a demanding question is: which takes higher priority, the greatest happiness or the greatest number?

Suppose just three people, Aimee, Ariadne and Ardon. Perhaps Ardon has far greater happiness potential than the two women combined; Aimee and Ariadne should therefore forgo their happiness, with resources heading to Ardon – maybe the women become his slaves – causing him immense happiness, swamping the women's unhappiness. Greatest happiness is thus secured. If, though, the greatest *number* of happy individuals takes highest priority, then – and here is a second scenario – Ardon should forgo happiness, serving as overworked slave to the two women; the two women each have maximum happiness, though the trio's combined happiness is now lower than in the first scenario. A third version would seek an equal happiness distribution: the three would each have a reasonable and equal amount of happiness, but the overall total could well be lower than in the two earlier scenarios.

A fourth version of our threesome tale would have the three creating more and more people. That could maximize happiness, even though each individual possesses only slight overall happiness, perhaps because of overcrowding. To avoid that fourth scenario, utilitarians may aim to maximize *average* happiness. Even if creating more people increases total happiness, the average happiness of the larger population could well be lower than that of the smaller population. The 'average' answer suffers a simple but significant fault: killing those whose happiness is below the current average, or below a certain level, could increase average happiness. Whether the increase occurs depends on whether and how such killings affect the remainder's happiness levels. The remainder may feel insecure at such killings, lowering overall happiness; some will find that their happiness is now below the new average, making them vulnerable to such a policy for increasing average happiness.

Distribution of a promoted good affects the amount of good for each individual, as does seeking the maximum good. Maximizing happiness, utilitarian-style, as sole concern, ignores whether the happiness amount for a given individual is good enough for that individual. Individuals seem mere containers for happiness; whether one container holds more happiness than another is ignored, unless affecting overall happiness. That some happiness is *my* happiness is irrelevant; it could be mixed in with the happiness of all others in one happiness-maximizing cauldron. That approach generates unease; what is morally right depends in part, it seems, upon how things are for each individual – and how lives compare.

Concern for the individual links with the mantra that individuals deserve to be treated equally – 'all men are equal' – but once 'what is deserved' is in the frame, we place limits on equality; equality in this or that respect should not be promoted. Ardon surely does not deserve as many resources as the others if he lazes while Aimee and Ariadne labour. Fairness, though, does not always merit highest priority. Suppose our three As are clinging to the wreckage of a shipwreck, with clean water scarce; equal water distribution would ensure all three perish. Fairness, it appears, yields to ensuring that at least one survives, however unfair that is for the others; but which of the three should survive – the owner of the ship, the owner of the water or the one who has so far had the least out of life? Should it be settled by a random draw? Utilitarians, presumably, would select the survivor as the one likely to generate the greatest happiness.

Mill sees maximum happiness as arising through individuals being free to develop as they choose, so long as not directly causing others to be harmed. The value of liberty becomes prominent in Mill's reasoning, as does the value of diversity – of society avoiding conformity to an overall uniformity. Mill speaks of

> a State, which dwarfs its men, in order that they may be more docile instruments in its hands even for beneficial purposes – will find that with small men no great thing can really be accomplished.

It has been argued, though, that the greatest happiness could result from people living in uniformity, following the crowd, even indoctrinated with mistaken beliefs. Mill's promotion of liberty could be at odds with his utilitarianism.

Mill can rightly reject such objections; happiness for Mill, it seems, essentially involves values such as knowing the truth, being autonomous (self-governing), honourable, imaginative and different. Mill's happiness, as already noted, is a flourishing or 'living well'. Mill also recognizes the importance of different conceptions of happiness; hence, his utilitarianism promotes conditions – public welfare – that would enable people to experiment with their chosen ways of living and, to use Adam Smith's expression, overcome 'the poverty of aspiration'. We should, though, beware such promotion collapsing into unquestioned praise for self-realization: 'to thy own self be true'. Caveats are needed for, of course, sincerity does not immunize us from wickedness. A murderer may be a sincere self-realizing murderer, an idler authentic in his sloth.

Urging greatness leads to competition. In competitions, some are hurt; some are swamped with envy, haughtily dismissed by the successful. The novelist Julian Barnes, commenting on the annual Booker (now Man Booker) Prize for fiction, noted:

JOHN STUART MILL: DISCOVERING THE CHARM

John Stuart Mill (1806–73), home-educated, was learning classical Greek from age three, then Latin, then correcting his father's six volumes on British India. Much influenced by Bentham, close family friend, Mill, in his teens, formed the Utilitarian Society. The term 'utilitarian' had appeared in Galt's novel *Annals of the Parish*. Mill, 'with a boy's fondness for a name and a banner', was the first to describe himself, and others, thus.

Ceasing to charm: At twenty, Mill asked himself about his aims:

> Suppose that all your objects in life were realized; that all the changes in institutions and opinions which you are looking forward to, could be completely effected at this very instant: would this be a great joy and happiness to you?

He answered 'No!' – a mental malady. 'The end had ceased to charm.'

Charm rediscovered: Mill came to see that happiness involved more than Benthamite pleasures. He discovered Wordsworth's poetry, nature's beauty and the love of Harriet Taylor – a pity she was *Mrs* Taylor. Respecting her husband, Harriet and John lived apart for twenty years, without impropriety. Their relationship, wrote Harriet, gave

> an edifying picture for those poor wretches who cannot conceive friendship but in sex – nor believe that expediency and the consideration for the feelings of others can conquer sensuality.

Bentham would, no doubt, have disagreed.

After Mr Taylor's death, John and Harriet married. True to his advocacy of equality, John disclaimed rights over Harriet and her property. With Harriet's death seven years later, John was heartbroken. He purchased a small white house in Avignon, installing the furniture from the nearby hotel room, scene of her death. The house overlooked the cemetery where she was buried. From 8 May 1873, the house overlooked the cemetery where, side by side, Harriet and John were buried.

Eminent Victorian reformer, Mill was greatly respected – a Member of Parliament, promoter of liberty, equality and welfare, even arguing against the mistreatment of horses. Mill felt sympathy, empathy, fellow-feeling – and, eventually, personal love. He was, after all, human.

The Booker... is beginning to drive people mad. It drives publishers mad with hope, booksellers mad with greed, judges mad with power, winners mad with pride, and losers (the unsuccessful shortlistees plus every other novelist in the country) mad with envy and disappointment.

On the bigger scale, Mill accepted the beneficial effects of business competition, yet with competition, some people suffer through losing the competitive race, being driven out of business. Overall, though, happiness gains – so it is believed.

Equality and fairness in distribution are not the sole values that challenge utilitarian reasoning. Numerous scenarios exist in which utilitarians seem committed to apparent immoralities. Here are some...

Justice dictates that only the guilty merit punishment, but suppose a community has suffered violent assaults, rapes and murders. The locals are convinced that a particular 'outsider' is the criminal. The authorities know of his total innocence – the real perpetrator recently committed suicide – but they also know that the community distrusts them and would dismiss their evidence of suicide. The public remains terrified while the outsider remains free. For utilitarians, it would surely be right for the authorities to falsify evidence, ensuring that the innocent outsider is convicted, incarcerated, even put to death. True, he would have a miserable time or no time at all; but the community's relief would easily outweigh that. 'So much for justice,' declare objectors to utilitarianism.

The 1666 Great Fire of London destroyed much of the City. Fingers pointed at Robert Hubert as the arsonist – an outsider, a simpleton. Although he was not the fire-raiser (being out of England at the time), a jury found him guilty and he was hanged. Justice was not done, but riots were probably avoided. Utilitarians should applaud the outcome. The people's satisfaction, though, derived from their belief that the culprit had been *rightfully* punished; they possessed a belief in justice, distinct from utilitarian morality. That thought points to Government House utilitarianism (please see insert, 'Utilitarianism in secret', p. 35).

Honesty, promise-keeping, even life preservation – all these may come under pressure if utilitarian justifications hold sway. Promise-keeping, for example, is, as with guilt, essentially 'backward looking' – not in its being regressive, but its regard for what *was* done. Marisa takes out a loan voluntarily, promising repayment next year. Morally, she ought to repay – our typical moral stance – yet circumstances could easily be described whereby the greatest happiness would result if she broke the promise.

Must we calculate the common welfare before kissing?

Everyday morality readily recognizes values other than overall happiness – for example, fairness, justice, equality, honesty, respecting human life. Utilitarians have three responses. One is to shore up the basic utilitarian line with explanations of how, properly understood, utilitarianism grounds those other values. The second response supplements or nuances the theory. A third line, described in the next section, produces radical revisions.

Taking the first line, we could argue that, as a matter of fact, people would feel insecure and worried if they ran the risk of being punished although innocent, or treated as human organ plantations for community benefit. That would be a utilitarian justification for resisting the lure of such seemingly immoral proposals, unless the proposals could be applied in secret, ensuring the ignorance of others. Regarding promise-keeping and honesty: well, if people know that utilitarian calculations could sometimes justify dishonesty and breaking promises, they would not rely so readily on them; that would create insecurity, chaos, thus, thwarting happiness being maximized.

There are problems with the above utilitarian remedies. Even if dishonesty, promise-breaking and killing people for their organs would have adverse overall consequences, that is not, many would argue, why such actions are morally wrong. Those actions are wrong whatever the consequences – a claim to be met in the next chapter.

Instead of sticking firmly with basic utilitarianism, we may follow the second proposed line – of nuancing the theory. Utilitarians can rightly draw distinctions between the overall desirable utilitarian end, people's individual motivations, the principles people should follow day by day – and the character traits to be encouraged. Mill notes, for example, that we sense the need to treat the interests of others equally, that we value social co-operation; maximizing happiness will hence require such relationships and characteristics to flourish. Yes, the overall end remains maximum happiness, but, to achieve that, we should often be motivated by love, by respect for others for their sake. Our eyes need to be shielded from the utilitarian end.

John Austin, a one-time close utilitarian friend of Mill, quipped that a man should not consult the common weal, the common welfare, before kissing his mistress: to do so would undermine the loving relationship and hence happiness. How would we feel were people to perform utilitarian calculations, or any calculations at all, before kissing us – or before keeping promises? Non-calculative loving relationships are usually part of people's happiness. Utilitarianism hence needs to be self-effacing – out of mind – where everyday motivations are concerned. A related current example are 'prenuptial contracts'; when suggested, they can undermine prospects for loving relationships.

Even in circumstances where calculations can coexist with happiness, it may be impractical to perform them. Hence, on utilitarian grounds, we need to develop certain rules of thumb, as well as character traits, of honesty, promise-keeping and generosity. By doing so, happiness will be advanced.

The above thinking can be viewed as an 'indirect utilitarianism', one that pulls us away from applying utilitarian calculations to every proposed act.

Rule utilitarianism: what if everyone...?

Utilitarians, as shown above, seek to avoid counter-intuitive results, either by insisting that proper calculations do not lead to the undesirable results or by nuancing the theory to avoid those results. A third move effects a radical transformation – into the indirect version of rule utilitarianism.

Act utilitarianism asks, 'Will this particular action maximize happiness?' The nuances above retain that basic principle, but recognize that motivations may differ from ultimate ends sought; and certain dispositions and rules of thumb are valuable for day-by-day navigation. *Rule* utilitarians do not apply utilitarian reasoning directly to a proposed act, but ask, 'Were (hypothetically) everyone, when in similar circumstances, to perform actions of this *type*, would happiness be maximized?' Rule utilitarians move us from actual to hypothetical consequences – those consequences resulting on the hypothesis of universal rule-following.

Suppose the following is true: if people stopped eating meat, then overall happiness would increase. There would be radically less animal suffering and people would probably lead healthier lives. There could be more efficient use of land for crops: fewer people would suffer malnourishment. Those advantages in total outweigh the initial misery of meat-eaters deprived of their meat-eating pleasures, and the loss of any pleasures of farmed animals unaware of forthcoming abattoir trips. With that as background, you are now in the supermarket, wanting to buy some veal. The choice is between veal and vegetarian.

Act utilitarians could justifiably recommend the veal. The creature is already dead; you will gain pleasure from the forthcoming meal – and, vitally, your purchase, be it for veal or vegetarian, will make no significant impact on others' purchasing behaviour and the supermarket's profits. The reasoning would be different, were you a charismatic, highly influential celebrity or admired political or religious leader; then, proclaiming vegetarianism and acting accordingly could lead numerous others to follow suit. That would affect supermarket buying policies, with resultant reductions in factory farming and animal suffering.

By contrast, rule utilitarians reason as follows: what if everyone were to do the same type of action as I do in these circumstances? If I resist the veal and go for the vegetarian meal, then, were everyone to behave similarly, there would be greater overall happiness than if they followed the rule of purchasing meat whenever they fancied. Even though my vegetarian choice in fact will make no difference to animal suffering – I am no charismatic celebrity – the vegetarian choice is what morality demands. The choice secures maximum happiness, were everyone to follow the same rule: buy vegetarian dishes, not meat.

Much moral reasoning seems rule utilitarian. In an election, my vote typically makes no difference to the electoral outcome. An act utilitarian may argue: I ought to do something more useful or pleasurable than voting. 'But what if everyone thought that way and ceased to vote?' people reply. The notice in the park says, 'Do not pick the flowers' – but if I picked and no one followed suit, the floral display would remain stunning. 'But what if everyone picked the flowers whenever it suited him or her? – no longer would there be the park's flowery delights.' And so forth…

Act utilitarians will often encourage actions, even though, were everyone to follow suit, happiness reduction would flow. Act utilitarians confidently reply, 'Not everyone will follow suit.' Rule utilitarians dismiss that reply; they see morality as founded in best rules. Best rules are determined by the 'what if everyone…' test; the rules typically coincide with common sense morality. If everyone lied when it suited him or her, there would be chaos; so, follow the rule: be honest. If we all broke the law whenever we could get away with it, society would collapse; hence, obey the law.

One mystery with rule utilitarianism is the justification behind each rule promoted. Perhaps 'only pick the flowers when few people are likely to notice the outcome' would be a better rule for happiness maximization than the blanket: do not pick the flowers. 'Always stop at red traffic lights except when clearly no other vehicles are crossing' could be better than: never cross red lights. Consider truth-telling: why restrict the rule choice solely between 'always tell the truth' and 'lie whenever it suits you'? Perhaps a better rule than either would be: tell the truth, unless lying would prevent a murder. Perhaps better still: tell the truth, unless it would reduce overall happiness. That latter rule would justify lying to your dying parents, not worrying them about your chaotic life. The rule utilitarian response could be: if that seemingly better rule became generally known, then we should not know whether to believe people; so, happiness would not be maximized. Perhaps rule utilitarianism, though, could operate with some degree of self-deception or acceptance of truthfulness 'for the most part' – or at least with more complex rules than the simple 'black or white' proposals.

Rule utilitarianism, in fact, risks collapse into act utilitarianism; the rules could be made so complicated that they enjoin the same actions as those of act utilitarianism. The collapse is avoided if a constraint is introduced: for example, the rules must be very simple and easy to follow. On particular occasions, though, rule utilitarians may well know that to maximize happiness they should break the relevant rules, yet their rule utilitarianism commits them to following the simple rules. That is an unhappy outcome and, one may add, not psychologically all that healthy.

Utilitarianism, act and rule, is vulnerable to a fundamental attack. Take an extreme case. 'It is wrong to torture this child for sheer fun.' Why? Act utilitarians rely on overall happiness being diminished – but is that really why such torture is wrong? Rule

UTILITARIANISM IN SECRET

Henry Sidgwick (1838–1900), unlike Bentham and Mill, was an academic, a leading Cambridge professor and reformer, promoting, for example, university education for women.

The need for secrecy: Utilitarians, Sidgwick argues, understand morality correctly. The greatest happiness, though, is unlikely to result if most people are aware of morality's utilitarian basis; they could spend ages calculating outcomes or, more likely, miscalculating. Perhaps they would doubt morality, if realizing it is not divinely commanded; they could then succumb to blatant selfishness.

Government House utilitarianism: Sidgwick concludes that the desirable end, happiness maximization, agreeable consciousness, is most likely secured if most people are convinced there exist firm moral principles that must be followed, regardless of consequences. Only the enlightened few should know of morality's utilitarian basis; they are akin to European rulers in the Government House of a colony. Sidgwick writes:

> On Utilitarian principles, it may be right to do and privately recommend, under certain circumstances, what it would not be right to advocate openly...

It may be right secretly to frame an innocent man for the greater good. That people ought sometimes to be ignorant is summarized pithily in Gore Vidal's comment, 'Never give the game away.' It is justified, not so pithily, in Plato's *Republic*'s defence of the 'noble lie', where rulers lie for a community to run well.

Keeping secrecy secret: Sidgwick, ever consistent, concludes: 'that the opinion that secrecy may render an action right which would not otherwise be so, should itself be kept comparatively secret...'

Was Sidgwick right to publish that view? Surely, it should be kept secret. Well, it is tucked away in his long and dusty *Methods of Ethics*; perhaps, he guessed, few readers would read that far in.

utilitarians argue that if we followed the rule 'torture children whenever you feel like doing so', overall happiness would diminish. Is that 'what if' consideration really the reason why torture is wrong? Even were there no decrease in overall happiness through such torturing – torturers gain immense pleasure – torture would surely remain morally repugnant, morally wrong.

The infamous 'Jim and the Indians'

Concern for the individual may be swallowed up by the utilitarian quest for total happiness. We noted earlier a tension between concern for the community and concern for the individual, as Mill's gaze turned from the greatest happiness to individuals' liberty. We now look more closely at the individual. Morality affects me as an agent, as someone who acts. It is self-directed in that *I* perform the action, though it is not thereby self-interested; I may see that I must act in the interest of others. As an agent, what *I* morally ought to do is not, it seems, determined solely by overall happiness.

Here is Bernard Williams's vivid tale of Jim finding himself in a South American village. Tied up against the wall are twenty terrified Indians, randomly selected. Because of recent anti-government protests, Pedro, an army officer, is about to shoot these innocents dead – to remind future possible protestors of the advantages of not protesting. A captain is in charge.

> Since Jim is an honoured visitor from another land, the captain is happy to offer him a guest's privilege of killing one of the Indians himself. If Jim accepts, then as a special mark of the occasion, the other Indians will be let off. Of course, if Jim refuses, then there is no special occasion, and Pedro here will do what he was about to do when Jim arrived, and kill them all... What should Jim do?

There is no chance of Jim turning the tables against Pedro and the captain. The twenty men against the wall – and their families – beg Jim to accept the offer.

Act utilitarians would see no moral dilemma: Jim should shoot one of the Indians. Rule utilitarians could come to see that following the simple rule 'do not kill' would be silly and cruel; better the rule: do not kill unless the individual to be killed is about to be killed in any case and other lives will be saved. Jim, though, would be the killing agent – using an Indian as a means to save the others. Even though the right action could well be to shoot, none the less it is morally significant to Jim that *he* would become a killer; he cannot see the act as agent-neutral. Killing could be so morally repulsive for him that he would not be true to himself if he went ahead. The 'view from here' of one agent – of Jim, if so repulsed – and the 'view from there' of someone else may differ.

The example raises the 'integrity' objection to utilitarianism. Consequences are important, but so is the integrity of the agent who brings forth those consequences. 'Let me keep my hands clean' – but that can smack of moral self-indulgence, even cowardice. Perhaps Jim's hands would be sullied by *not* shooting. He would feel terrible at killing; but maybe killing is what he ought to do. Were another explorer to be present, Jim, while refusing the killing to be done 'through me', could yet be hoping that the other explorer would accept the captain's offer. That hope does not sit well with Jim as a man of integrity, even though, given their priorities, it is morally wrong for him to kill, yet right for someone else to kill, someone whose integrity would remain unimpeached by killing.

The scenario presents a simplified choice for Jim. If, though, truly horrified by the plight of all twenty innocent Indians, Jim may feel unable to live with himself if he accepts – or declines – the offer. Either way, he would be enmeshed in tragedy not of his making. He may seek a noble path, sincerely offering up his own life to save the twenty, perhaps hoping that such an offer of self-sacrifice would touch the captain's heart, leading to all being saved.

Integrity is a recognizable value – one that homes in on agents being true to their principles. Integrity, let us remember, does not, though, always merit highest priority, even any priority. Some Nazis, 'true to their principles', went ahead with killing innocent Jews trembling before their eyes.

There are cases where involvement in a cause would secure recognizable overall benefits. You have the opportunity to infil- trate an undesirable political grouping intent on attacking racial minorities. As a member, you would learn of its plans, your ultimate aim being to disrupt its activities. The benefits of infiltration are there to see; yet although some people would hence infiltrate, you could not live with yourself becoming 'one of them' – and living in the public gaze as one of them. Is that putting 'self' first, over-concerned about appearances – or a proper moral reflection, regarding the sort of person you are?

The twentieth-century British spies – the 'Cambridge Spies' – spied for Soviet communism and against fascism. To move high within the British secret services and be trusted by the Americans, their cover involved appearing right-wing. As a result, they lost important political friendships and loves, for what they perceived to be the greater good. They sacrificed their personal lives for a political value. Here is another example: Alan Turing and col- leagues, engaged in cracking the Enigma Code during World War II, maintained their work's secrecy; they received white feathers from women who thought them cowards for not being in the forces, fighting for their country. They lived with that public dishonour, while behaving honourably.

Agent centrality, of actions being *mine*, has moral significance. A person's character and what gives substance to his life are morally relevant to how he should act. Morality is not concerned solely with overall consequences, detached from the agent. Further morally relevant partialities are generated by personal relationships; here is an example.

Consider lover-ism: is there anything wrong in giving preference to your beloved? Whom you serve in a shop should surely not rest on race, sex or love, but surely with whom you sleep or dine can rest on such factors. Impartiality is not required there. A classic example is that of 'whom to save?' A woman is able to save only one individual from drowning, yet two individuals are in the water, one her husband, the other unknown. Would the woman be guilty of prejudice, of marriage-ism, of love-ism, in choosing automatically to save her husband? Should she choose whom to save on the basis of maximizing overall happiness? Even to think about it may, in Bernard Williams's observation, be 'one thought too many'.

That personal relationships are highly relevant to morality may account for the difference between the moral demands on governmental authorities and those on individuals. Medical authorities may rightly refuse the provision of certain treatments, knowing that they are ineffective or wildly costly for what may be achieved. We can understand, though – morally understand – how the mother of a dying child may do virtually anything to secure that treatment for her son, 'just in case'; we can also understand – morally understand – how another mother, equally compassionate, may reluctantly accept that nothing can be done.

Although utilitarianism finds it difficult to cope with partialities introduced by integrity – as revealed in 'Jim and the Indians' – perhaps it does not have to falter when faced with relational partialities. Biologically constituted as we are, maximum happiness could well result if certain feelings and spontaneous actions – regarding one's own children, for example – are nurtured. The objection to that utilitarian response is that, in a particular situation, act utilitarians theoretically ought seriously to wonder whom to save – it can sometimes be better to override spontaneous feelings – and rule utilitarians, even with complicated rules prioritizing family and lovers, would still be applying rules, engaging one thought, or many thoughts, too many.

We naturally feel that a mother should save her child from drowning rather than an unknown other. To act otherwise would be inhuman. Utilitarianism's support for that natural feeling hangs solely on whether maximum happiness results. Utilitarians must be open to the possibility of overall happiness arising, for example, if the community brings up children, making them unaware of their biological parents. Promoters of the Jewish kibbutz, at one time, supported communal child-rearing, as did Plato in his *Republic* regarding children of the ruling guardians.

For utilitarians, which partialities merit promotion is determined by global happiness-maximizing. Others see moral value in some partialities irrespective of overall happiness. An extreme partiality is simple self-interest, in conflict with much of common morality. Partialities can, though, fan out and blossom, and usually do: parents embrace the interests of their children; villagers of their village; nationals of their own nation; and individuals of their own ethnic groups. Witness, though, the political promotion of 'looking after our own' that hampers a wider moral gaze. Morally, we typically feel comfortable with some partialities, but not others; so, how should lines be drawn? What justifies exclusion from our moral circles?

$$\gamma$$

Let us then review another incredibly influential moral theory relevant to these puzzles. It emphasizes the importance of what we, the agents, intend, while maintaining two key similarities with utilitarianism: universality and impartiality. We are approaching Kant's deontological theory, a theory that can appear austere. It is vastly removed from pleasures, be they egoistic, utilitarian, higher or lower. The watchword is 'duty'.

3
Deontology: 'I must not tell a lie'

'I cannot tell a lie' – George Washington reputedly said, aged six. Whether Washington did or did not tell a lie, no doubt he could have told lies. Most people readily accept that, although we can tell lies, there is something wrong in lying: we must not – we ought not to – lie. Curiously, many rest more easily with being 'economical with the truth', even though the outcome can mislead as readily as straight lies. Most of us sometimes lie, either defending the lies as 'little white lies' or as avoidance of worse wrongs – or with no good justification at all, save feebleness in facing the truth.

'Do not lie' is one duty, a negative duty, prescribing what *not* to do. We can avoid telling the truth by lapsing into silence, doing no telling at all. 'Do not kill, torture or steal' gives voice to other negative duties. A positive duty is to come to the aid of those whose lives are in danger. Caveats are usually added. Most people are lying when they sign documents, confirming they have read terms and conditions in the small print; but does that count as immoral? Many people, Immanuel Kant included, insist that capital punishment – killing murderers – after a just legal process is not merely permissible, but obligatory.

Many accept the duties just mentioned. Utilitarians, as seen, try to harmonize their approach, at least to some degree, with such common sense morality – acting in accord with those duties may maximize happiness – but it is Kant, the great Enlightenment philosopher, who sought to provide rational groundings to such duties. He is central to deontological ethics – 'deon' meaning *one must*. Deontologists promote certain duties. Were that the essence of deontological ethics – as is casually supposed – utilitarianism would be a deontology: utilitarians insist that our duty is to maximize happiness. Deontology, though, is usually contrasted with consequentialist approaches such as utilitarianism. Deontological morality, as typically understood, lacks regard for an action's overall consequences; well, that is the line propounded. Some actions are wrong, are morally prohibited, even if overall outcomes would be splendidly good. Further, moral duties hold fast for each agent: duties do not depend on how they impinge upon the moral duties of others. Here is an example.

Killing an innocent man is wrong – full stop. It is wrong even if, through my not killing *this* innocent man, many innocent individuals are killed by others; that immorality belongs to the others. Their immorality does not taint me. If 'do not kill' is indeed one moral duty, then Jim (recall 'Jim and the Indians') ought not to kill, even though the outcome is bad, with Pedro killing the twenty captive Indians. Jim's hands are morally clean, despite the known consequences, despite him, in a sense, letting the twenty die. Some fancy footwork or casuistry – some subtle reasoning intended to rationalize or perhaps mislead – is needed here to ensure that there is a morally relevant distinction between killing and letting die. Had he taken up the offer to shoot a captive, he would have intended a death; in declining the offer, he intended no deaths, though he foresaw twenty. He is not to blame for the happenings that he foresaw (please see 'double effect', p.58). Of course, that does not help the twenty doomed captives.

Deontological morality demands that we do the right thing even if good does not result. The *right*, so to speak, wears the trousers; the *right* takes priority over the *good*. My duty has regard solely to *my* doing the right thing – acting according to the relevant moral maxim, the moral principle that I endorse – even if the result is that another, or many others, fail in their duties.

Deontologists are under no obligation to maximize the number of right actions. Paradoxically, according to deontological ethics it is not morally permissible for me to do something wrong, even if it would prevent numerous wrongs being performed by others.

Categorical Imperative: the wonder of the moral law

Immanuel Kant is no easy writer to read, whether in his original German or in English translation. Native German speakers have been known to find the English translations easier to understand; hence, unsurprisingly, interpretations of Kant's ethics vary. Pretty constant, though, is Kant's image as a stern and unbending moralist.

'Two things fill me with wonder,' proclaimed Kant, 'the starry sky above and the moral law within.' Moral demands are not grounded in consequences or happiness or our biological contingencies:

> My worth as an intelligence is raised infinitely by my being a person in whom the moral law reveals to him a life independent of all animality, and even of the whole world of sense.

Moral behaviour is a demand of reason; and reason, for Kant, is tied intrinsically to autonomy, self-government, not to emotions. We are focusing here on persons, on human beings as rational agents, rather than as entities of nature at the mercy of biological urges. Reason leads us to Kant's Categorical Imperative, morality's heart. Let us see what this means.

Imperatives are orders: pour another drink; turn off the mobile – but those imperatives are conditional on certain desires, needs or aims. If you desire intoxication – on that condition – well, pour another drink. I need peace and quiet, so turn off the mobile. If they were categorical imperatives, they would hold universally, for one and all, independently of contingent desires. The bizarre conclusions, in those examples, would be that everyone must have another drink and have peace and quiet (mind you, this author would support the latter as a state of unintruded bliss).

A categorical imperative lacks contingent conditions: it has built within both universality and impartiality; it applies to all equally, impartially. Arithmetical truths, $2 + 2 = 4$, hold the same throughout the universe, whether in Great Britain, China or on Mars – whether one is black, white, Chinese or Martian. Moral duties, being based on reason, also hold universally, impartially – unconditionally – insisted Kant. We may be forgiven for believing, then, that the utilitarian demand must be a categorical imperative. Indeed, without using that terminology, utilitarians clearly think that is so: the 'maximize happiness' imperative is not conditional. Kant rejects that imperative, as we shall see.

Kant's Categorical Imperative grounds all morality. It is usually treated as revealed in three versions; they are meant to amount to the one imperative. Here is Kant's Formula of Universal Law:

> Act only on that maxim through which you can at the same time will that it should become a universal law.

A maxim, to be morally acceptable, must pass this universalizing test. The test harmonizes with the common cry, 'What if everyone behaved that way?' – a cry encountered already within rule utilitarianism. Let us see how the test works, and hence differs from rule utilitarianism, before considering why it should be thought to be morality's grounding.

The universal and the general are distinct; the general is a matter of degree. Kant sought laws that are universal, applying to everybody everywhere, impartially, untied to any particular individual; he also wanted them to be pretty general. A universal law with little generality would be 'never shoot anybody who wears a hat and yellow socks'. A more general law, yet not with Kantian universality because tied to a particular, would be: everyone must give Miranda, *that* particular woman, whatever she wants. If applying to all, 'do not lie' is impartial, but that accolade may mislead; it is a greater burden on would-be liars than non-liars.

Here is Kant's most promising example of the formula in operation, one that, as it happens, concerns promises.

I borrow some money, explicitly promising to repay, yet I have no intention of doing so. My personal maxim, the rule that I apply, is that of promising while intending to break the promise (hereafter, a 'lying promise'). How does that maxim stand according to the Formula of Universal Law? To answer, turn the maxim into a universal law – a law of nature, as Kant describes it – whereby everyone follows the personal maxim of making lying promises. Could I rationally will that state of affairs to exist?

Kant answers 'no' – it would be irrational to accept promises, if promises universally were not to be kept. The idea of universal lying promises is contradictory in its very conception; the institution of promising could not exist. Passing the formula's test is, though, a necessary condition for a maxim to be moral. Thus, making promises with no intention of keeping them is ruled out; it is immoral. Similar reasoning leads to the more general conclusion that lying and dishonesty are immoral. The Categorical Imperative has revealed some negative duties – what we must *not* do.

The reasoning is not intended to succeed on the basis that we would not *want* to universalize the maxim, or that it would be imprudent to do so. Were it to succeed on that basis, it would be conditional on contingent desires – desires that we just happen to have – or on rule utilitarian consequentialist considerations. Kant's test determines whether a contradiction arises. Hence his Categorical Imperative differs from the Golden Rule, found in Confucius, in St Matthew's Gospel and elsewhere, namely: do unto others as you would have them do unto you. The Golden Rule could be an appeal to self-interest or to fairness; we should

IMMANUEL KANT: THE DIGNITY OF HUMANITY

Immanuel Kant (1724–1804), born in Königsberg, remained in the Königsberg locality all his life. Had he died early, in his fifties, he would have died an unknown professor at an undistinguished university in an undistinguished German town. By the 1780s, though, his major *Critiques* were appearing; he gained international fame as a remarkable and admired Enlightenment philosopher, to be placed beside Plato and Aristotle.

Crooked timber of humanity: Kant rejected his Lutheran, Pietistic, upbringing, with its biblical appeals, but kept its stress on our thinking for ourselves, an Enlightenment impulse. He was struck by how morality binds us: people can recognize their duties and the 'beauty and dignity of human nature'. Such is not the province solely of philosophers.

Kant was also struck by institutional injustices – of labourers suffering lives of hard work, contrasting with wealthy lives that can lead the wealthy into selfishness and disrespect for the poor. Thus, Kant spoke of 'the crooked timber of humanity'.

Slipping a tip: Kant thought moral duty must be carried out for its own sake; yet happiness, as the highest good, is deserved by those morally strong enough to perform their duties. Happiness depends on God's salvific will, on his grace. Schopenhauer quipped, 'That is akin to slipping a tip to a head-waiter when pretending to be above such things.'

Universal dignity: Arguing for the dignity of, and respect due, to all people – an unconditional egalitarianism – Kant saw it as an impersonal principle rather than as an urging to enjoy people's individualities. Over his own writings, he quoted sixteenth-century Francis Bacon, 'About ourselves we are silent'. He had regard for socializing, though, favouring good meals in good company – with jokes.

The 'disinterested interest' of moral respect, he strangely termed 'the courtesy of the heart'. A few days before his death – very ill, almost blind – Kant rose when his doctor entered, waiting for the doctor to be seated before following suit. He was pleased to note of himself:

The sense of humanity has not abandoned me.

need to universalize and specify some doings to assess how things stand regarding the Categorical Imperative.

Even Kant's 'best case' – the rejection of lying promises – has problems. There need be no contradiction in lying promises being universal, for people may not know that others follow the lying promise maxim, or they may be irrational enough not to grasp its consequences. The test requires all players to be well-informed rational agents. Let us assume such supplementation applies; and let us turn to another Kantian example, one that locates the contradiction in the willing rather than the conception of what is willed.

Consider a man in despair, weary of life, contemplating suicide. Could the personal maxim of killing oneself – a 'principle of self-love', of prudence – become a universal law of nature? The maxim universalized is:

> For love of myself, I make it my principle to cut my life short when prolonging it threatens to bring more troubles than satisfactions.

There could not be a rational willing of such a universal law, insists Kant, for nature would be contradicting itself; hence, suicide is morally wrong. Although the reasoning mentions the prudent, Kant argues that the immorality arises because of a contradiction in the willing itself. His reasoning, though, is obscure. There certainly is no contradiction of conception in universal suicide; it is logically possible that everyone commits suicide or – to include a related maxim for consideration – seeks to kill others. Contrast that with the would-be lying promiser; he sees success crumbling were lying promising universalized.

Kant's world was pre-Darwinian; his claim that there is a contradiction in the suicide's willing depends upon nature being teleological, that is, possessed of purposes. That world is alien to many of us today: people have purposes; nature does not. Staying with Kant's view, the contradiction in willing universal suicide occurs because nature's purpose of life preservation clashes with the suicides' life destruction. There exists a contradiction, or at least an irrationality, in willing universal suicide out of self-love, given the natural purpose of self-love, of life preservation. The universalizing test here, though, appears unnecessary: any irrationality would arise with just one individual willing suicide, given his self-love. To avoid that criticism, Kant would need to argue that nature's purpose is compatible with a particular individual suicide but not with someone willing universal suicide; it is that latter incompatibility that makes an individual suicide immoral.

Presumably Kant would also appeal to nature's purposes to show that enjoining enforced mass murder is an immoral maxim; yet surely such immorality does not rest on the maxim failing a universalizing test, be it because of nature's purposes or not.

For another example, let us try stealing, so to speak. The aim is to possess another's property. If the would-be thief wills the universal maxim – everybody to steal whenever he or she wants – tension arises in the willing. It would surely be irrational to will one's ownership of property (through theft), yet also will that property ownership not be respected: the thief would be willing that his property be exposed to theft. That line of reasoning could also show how killing others, while seeking one's own life preservation, is morally wrong. With the theft example, however, we may ask whether the institution of property ownership can be justified – after all, some, for instance, Pierre-Joseph Proudhon, perceive privately owned property to be theft. The Categorical Imperative is a poor guide regarding whether the institution of private property is morally acceptable. With life preservation, maybe no further justificatory question arises; life is not a conventional institution requiring justification, unlike property being privately owned.

The above discussion relates to negative duties. Kant also argues for the positive duty to help others. Kant tells of a man who recognizes the hardships of others, yet lacks all desire to help, thinking, 'Let each one be as happy as heaven wills, or as he can make himself.' Kant observes:

> If such a way of thinking were a universal law of nature, the human race could certainly survive… But a will that brought that about would conflict with itself, since instances can often arise in which the person would need the love and sympathy of others, and he would have no hope of getting the help he desires, being robbed of it by this law of nature springing from his own will.

The universalizing in the above shows only that his ignoring the plight of others could get in the way of his receiving help – but that sounds like self-love, a prudential concern. Certainly, on the surface, it is far removed from the lofty approach of Kantian duty.

The Categorical Imperative test rests on showing how the end sought in an individual case would be frustrated, were the desired action universalized. To secure our ends through dishonesty, lying or unfairness, we require the norm of people being honest, truthful and fair. To secure our ends through theft, killing and meanness, we require others to respect property and life – and to be helpful.

Is wicket-keeping, cricket – morally so?

Even if the reasoning regarding lying promises works – the most convincing application of the Categorical Imperative – it fails to show that the institution of promising is morally valuable: it shows that, if there is the institution, then there is a problem in universalizing lying promises. Were there the institution of bribery, we could add, there would be a problem in universalizing non-acceptance of bribes. Hence, the universalizing condition, until more is said, is insufficient to show that the institution under review is itself valuable. The universalizing requirement harmonizes, though, with some plausible thoughts. Perhaps there is something morally dubious about individuals who want to give but never receive, to love but never be loved, to have their promises accepted but never accept promises from others. Their moral dubiety, though, cannot be solely that they fail the Categorical Imperative test; lots of innocent acts also fail the test.

I play cricket only if I can be wicket-keeper. Were everyone to play cricket on that basis, there could be no cricket. I am a seller of hats, but never a buyer; were everyone to follow my maxim, there could be no buying or selling of hats. There is, though, nothing immoral in someone playing cricket only if he is a wicket-keeper, or selling but never buying hats. Were the Categorical Imperative test applied to states of affairs, not just actions, we should encounter more problems. Simply being the sole winner of this competition, the tallest woman, the eldest man, all logically require that others are not, yet surely there is immorality neither in such states, nor in seeking them. Failure to pass the Categorical Imperative test is not sufficient to show that the tested maxims are immoral. For actions to be morally permissible, it is not necessary for the related maxims to pass the test.

What should we make of maxims that do pass the test? I could will without contradiction that everyone wears a hat when outdoors, but hat-wearing is not an obvious moral matter and certainly is not universally morally obligatory. Is passing the test, though, sufficient to show that actions of a certain type are at least morally permissible? On the surface, the utilitarian aim of maximizing happiness could be willed universally, though presumably it would need to be reined in to exclude, for example, promise-breaking – or perhaps promise-keeping should be reined in, letting happiness maximization take higher priority. Committed anti-Semites could consistently universalize destruction of the Jews, accepting that if it transpired that they, the anti-Semites, were Jewish, they too should be destroyed – but that universal destruction is surely not morally permissible. Consistent universalizing fails to rule out such immoral partialities; thus, passing the

Categorical Imperative test does not guarantee that the proposed maxim and actions are morally acceptable.

Let us turn to a further possible immorality, one that focuses on an individual's treatment of himself. Kant argues that it is wrong to neglect our talents. Presumably he does not include talents for theft, rape or deceitful political spin; the resultant actions of such talents are no doubt excluded through application of the Categorical Imperative, as already discussed. Kant, though, tells of some South Pacific Islanders (allegedly) 'letting their talents rust and devoting their lives merely to idleness, indulgence, and baby-making – in short, to pleasure'. There is no contradiction in everyone disregarding his or her talents, promoting universal sloth; none the less, according to Kant, no one can rationally will such disregard to become a universal law of nature – but why?

Kant's reply is that 'a rational being necessarily wills that all his abilities should be developed, because they serve him and are given to him for all sorts of possible purposes'. It is difficult, though, to see how that derives from the Categorical Imperative, save through some mysterious purposes of nature.

In summary, passing the Categorical Imperative test fails to establish that the actions are morally permissible, let alone obligatory, and failing the test does not show the actions as immoral. Despite that, many feel that Kant is on to something. Maybe that something shines better when the universalizing focuses very much on people's autonomy, their freedom to act as they determine, to govern themselves. We step into autonomy.

The good will, sparkling like a jewel

Kant addresses people as rational autonomous agents; we can govern ourselves. We can override our biological urges, selfishness and personal ambitions; that governance is shown in our performance of moral duties. Kant places children, non-human animals, trees – pebbles, indeed – to one side and presumably also those suffering from senile dementia or similar. Those individuals are incapable of acting from duty; they fail to recognize, if they recognize at all, the distinction between wants and duties.

Most of us possess some awareness of moral duties and how they can conflict with wants, aims and possibly even with what is good for us. Moral duties cannot be determined by contingent facts about us, about what our desires happen to be, but must be determined by reason, applying to all. If Kant is right, then two points emerge. First, duty must be able to motivate us to act, to act morally. Secondly, biological urges that some have, but others lack, must not constitute the dutiful person's motivation. We could perhaps still accept that our reasoning rests on biology; but if so, it must rest on biological features essential to all rational agents.

Concerning the first point, human beings, because autonomous, are typically aware of, or can reason about, their moral duties. An unhappy paradox may emerge. People who fail to perform their duties must be lacking the relevant autonomy, the relevant reasoning – or, at least, their autonomy yields to various urges – but if they lack that autonomy or lack sufficiently strong autonomy, they no more merit moral blame than the tree whose bough breaks in the storm, striking passers-by.

That very picture of autonomy as rationality vying with desires had been challenged by David Hume, who claimed that reason is but a slave to the passions, to desires (please see p. 122). Hume argued that reason cannot tell us our aims; reason can only lead us to the best means for achieving our aims. Our aims and desires are grounded in our human nature.

Concerning the second point, consider two figures, Carrington and Cheryl, both encountering beggars in distress. Cheryl is emotionally moved; out of genuine concern, she gives them money, talks to them and tries to help. Carrington lacks such emotion; he views the beggars with disdain, yet, aware of his duty, gives some money. According to Kant, Carrington, not Cheryl, receives the moral credit. Biological luck fixed their different characters, not moral worth. Cheryl acted from her compassionate nature, blindly, slavishly; her action 'has no true moral worth, however amiable it may be and however much it accords with duty'. Carrington was driven by law-giving reason – by his good will.

Moral worth requires a good will; that is all. Just as contingent factors outside our control, such as biological constitution, should not affect moral worth, so too the contingencies of consequences, out of our control, are irrelevant. To quote Kant:

> Even if it should happen that, by a particularly unfortunate fate or by the niggardly provision of a step-motherly nature, the good will should be wholly lacking in power to accomplish its purpose, and if even the greatest effort should not avail it to achieve anything of its end, and if there remained only the good will (not as a mere wish but as the summoning of all the means in our power), it would sparkle like a jewel in its own right, as something with its full worth in itself.

Kant's understanding of moral behaviour leaves inexplicable why we often find certain feelings – remorse, dignity, shame – morally significant. It leaves inexplicable why we typically prefer people moved to help us because of our plight and not because of their thought: it's our duty. It makes mysterious why it is surely morally right that we feel grief at a friend's death and willingly attend the funeral, even if inconvenient.

We may also challenge Kant's understanding of morality as untouched by luck. Our grasp of Kant's moral law, it seems, depends on the luck of our upbringing and intellectual capacity grounded in neurology. People whose intellectual impoverishment amounts to lack of rationality appear to fall outside Kant's moral realm. That raises questions about how such individuals ought to be treated, questions raised regarding infants, dementia sufferers and, indeed, non-human animals.

THE MORALITY OF PUNISHMENT

Retribution: Law-breakers – when the laws are morally justified – deserve to be punished. That is, argues Kant, to treat them with respect, as moral agents, responsible for their actions. To punish criminals solely to deter people from crimes – a utilitarian stance – treats them merely as means to an end. The penal law is a categorical imperative:

> … and woe to him who creeps through the serpent-windings of utilitarianism to discover some advantage that may discharge him from the justice of punishment and its due measure… for if justice perishes, human life would no longer have value in the world.

Yes, punishment inflicts suffering on criminals, but that is not an offence against their autonomy, according to Kant.

Capital punishment: Justice must be done, even if no benefits result, for otherwise we should be participants in crime:

> Even if a civil society resolved to dissolve itself with the consent of all its members – as might be supposed if a people inhabiting an island resolved to separate and scatter themselves throughout the world – the last murderer lying in the prison ought to be executed before implementing the resolution.

Kant here relies on a principle of equality: a victim has suffered a loss, therefore the criminal must suffer an equivalent loss, maybe 'with interest', given that he broke the law – but what counts as 'equivalent'?

Penance: To inflict non-consensual suffering on criminals, even when no benefit results, strikes many as horrendous. Punishment 'cancelling out' the wickedness or 'balancing' the unjust benefits gained seems more 'nonsense on stilts', as Bentham would no doubt say.

What is wanted, we suggest, is for criminals to repent, feel remorse, eager to make amends. That involves suffering, but from the criminals' own grasp of their wrongdoings. It shows respect for the criminal and the victim – and has regard for securing consequential benefits. Of course, it is wildly ideal.

The Humanity Formula: respect for others

Duties not to kill, not to steal, have so far been derived from the Categorical Imperative's first presentation. It focuses on the general conditions – the form – that moral principles must satisfy; my willing to kill, willing to steal, would be ensnared in formal contradiction. There, autonomy is to the fore in considering what agents must or must not do: that is, their duties. Questions of autonomy also arise when people are possible victims of doings; indeed killings and theft are primarily seen as wrong because they violate others, their rights – the respect due to them. The Categorical Imperative's second presentation reveals the content of morality to be that very respect due to others. It is the Formula of the End in Itself, the Humanity Formula:

> We should treat humanity never simply as a means, but always at the same time as an end.

The universalizing test – the Formula of Universal Law – offers some support for the Humanity Formula: minimally, there exists some tension in my willing that I use others solely as a means to my ends, if that requires the possibility of my willing that everyone uses others similarly – for I should then be willing that I be treated solely as means to the ends of others. The universalizing test, though, generates problems for wicket-keepers, as we noted; the Humanity Formula does not. Fanatical anti-Semites perhaps act in a morally coherent way, according to the universalizing test; but they would clearly offend the Humanity Formula.

Let us look more closely at how we treat people. Most of us work for others, helping them to achieve their ends (sometimes, hindering). We are means to their ends, but not solely so; we have usually chosen the work voluntarily, taken on roles, to earn livings that are means to *our* ends. We are autonomous, self-governing, making our own choices. Of course, questions may be asked as to whether the work is truly voluntary if the sole alternative is starvation. Certainly when people are coerced into slavery or press-ganged into the navy, even if with payment, the slave-owners and captains would be using them merely as means – just as they may use horses to draw carts and waterfalls to turn wheels. Further, it is doubtful whether people's autonomy is respected today, when businesses and governments, via data collection and media outputs, manipulate people's desires and political beliefs. Indeed, are people being respected when 'mystery shoppers', police and regulators are permitted to lie to uncover wrongdoings?

Our moral intuitions summed as 'respect for people' are grounded in treating people as ends, not merely as, for example, units of wealth creation. We respect guests by standing, checkout staff by refraining from mobile phone use; we treat them as individuals with interests. More obviously within morality's arena, if we lie to people or cheat people, we lack respect for them. We are manipulating them, usually for our own ends. True, we sometimes lie, believing that ignorance is to people's blissful benefit; but perhaps autonomy always requires access to the truth.

Kant's promotion of respect does not sit happily with his insistence that duty alone should motivate morally. Respect for people, we may sense, requires feelings for their well-being; respecting people out of dispassionate duty sounds almost as paradoxical and unpleasant as befriending someone only if paid. Acknowledgement of people's autonomy can, though, be expressed as respect for people's rights; arguably, that respect can be coldly given. Respect for rights is often associated with the third presentation of Kant's Categorical Imperative, the Formula of the Kingdom of Ends:

> Every rational being must so act as if he were, through his maxims,
> a law-making member in the universal kingdom of ends.

The emphasis is on people as legislators, granting rights. Can our maxims, set out as people's rights, become universal laws of a Kingdom of Ends, a kingdom of rational agents? The approach polishes deontology with a 'contractualist' shine, the emphasis being on which laws can be justified rationally to each and every member of the community – for example, laws upholding rights to life, property and liberty. We meet approaches related to this line in Chapter Nine, when assessing the morality of political authority.

Conflicts

The Categorical Imperative, in all three forms, delivers certain obligatory moral maxims. There are bound, though, to be occasions when it is unclear how a maxim should be applied. Jim, in 'Jim and the Indians' (p. 36), must not kill, according to some. Jim respects the Indians by not killing any one of them. Is he really respecting them, though, by letting them all die? We have a distribution problem here: the distribution of respect. Only by disrespecting one – killing that one – is Jim, we may argue, respecting the remaining nineteen.

Kant apparently assumes that the Categorical Imperative delivers maxims that, together, are consistent. Abstractly, they may be; in particular circumstances, though, they could point in different directions. Are you obliged to keep your promise to return the sword to your friend this evening – an example from Plato – when you see that he has gone out of his mind and will harm himself with it?

> A terrorist uses an innocent child as a human shield, while he attempts to detonate a bomb. Only by killing the child can the detonation be prevented. Is that what you should do?

> A lorry driver is trapped in his cab, acid spilling over him, burning him, causing him horrendous pain. No escape is possible. He pleads to be shot dead. Should you shoot?

Should Kant's 'do not kill' maxim apply here? The examples raise questions of how actions should be described. Exactly what are you doing? Is shooting the driver understood correctly as killing him, or as relieving his pain? Consider, for example, the case where a physician delivers increased morphine to a patient terminally ill and in great suffering, a case maybe of assisted dying. He seeks to avoid the charge of murder:

> I intended the effect of reduced suffering – clearly a good. I fore-saw the patient's death – a bad. The death was a later unintended effect of what I did to achieve the good.

The Doctrine of Double Effect is being deployed: an agent is morally responsible for what he intends, but not thereby what he foresees as consequence, providing the intended effect is a sufficient good to make up, in some way, for the undesired, but foreseen, bad effect. The distinction is often used in law and theology. We may, though, doubt its moral significance when the agent – the doctor, in this case – knows of how closely related, causally, the two effects are. True, he may want only to relieve the pain and not cause the death, but if they are so entwined, and he knows that, it is disingenuous to deny his moral responsibility for the bad effect; he knowingly killed, even though he would have preferred non-fatal means to have relieved the suffering.

Returning directly to Kant, he addresses only one case of a seeming dilemma – that of whether to lie to a would-be murderer about his intended victim's whereabouts. Kant argues that so long as you adhere strictly to what you sincerely believe true, you cannot be blamed. If believing the victim to be indoors, you tell the murderer that he has left – well, says Kant, the victim may have slipped out unbeknownst to you and, by sheer misfortune, the murderer bumps into him and 'executes his purpose upon him'. You could then, with justice, be accused of causing the man's death.

Various replies to Kant are on offer. Sometimes we know that such bad luck will not arise: the victim cowers behind the door; we can see his shadow. We may also argue that a would-be murderer does not deserve the truth for such an immoral purpose. According to Kant, though, a lie always harms mankind. Mysteriously, lies, for Kant, are never morally permitted − well, so it seems.

Many people accept duties such as Kant's − we ought not to kill; ought not to lie; ought to help others − but they are seen as *prima facie* duties, duties at first sight, not absolute. The duties are real enough, but in particular cases they clash, needing judgement regarding highest priorities. Reflect on placebos prescribed to patients; patients benefit, for placebos can work and often with fewer side effects. Patients are, though, deceived, believing the pills to possess pharmaceutical powers. The mystery is: how do we judge which duties trump which − and when? We find a similar mystery in the next chapter, when weighing up different virtues.

Regarding the terrorist using a child as human shield, many would have the immediate intuition that the child morally ought not to be killed − certainly not, if just a few other lives are at risk. What if ten thousand will be killed − and it is certain that, if nothing is done, the terrorist will detonate? Such cases give rise to 'threshold deontology'. One obvious problem is how to determine the threshold. Is using a child solely as a means to an end acceptable if it will definitely save a million lives, but unacceptable if it will save only five? Here, as elsewhere, the belief that there must be numerical right answers is chimerical. Here, as elsewhere, we need to realize that sometimes whatever we do occasions some wrongdoing. Maybe here no good answers are possible until faced with the dilemma − or should governments, for example, keep torture equipment in reserve 'just in case', for one day it may be put to good use, revealing information that saves thousands of lives? That very question may make us recoil.

♈

Utilitarianism directs morality towards overall welfare, greatest happiness. Kant brings to the moral medley, among other things, 'respect for persons', never treating people solely as means, but as autonomous individuals with interests – that is, morality demands that we recognize the dignity of man, acknowledging that human beings merit the same rights as each other. Perhaps that is an ideal goal 'if only' we were all rational. According to Kant, it certainly matters that at least *I*, a rational agent, do not act immorally, even though the result may be that many others end up delivering immoralities. That agent centrality – what *I* do – was seen not to harmonize all that readily with utilitarianism's universality and impartiality. It also fails to harmonize well with Kant's own focus on universality and impartiality.

It is difficult to believe that a proper understanding of morality requires no reference to agent centrality – to which actions are my actions; to what gives substance to my life; to what can motivate me. Curious as it may seem, agent centrality takes centre stage when the moral spotlight turns to the virtues. Hence, it is to the virtues that we now turn.

4

Virtue ethics: a flourishing life

Do you admire a man who would rape and pillage if he could get away with it? Or a woman without scruples, who cheats and embezzles to climb the greasy pole, reaching the pinnacle of success? Do you respect parents who, without a care, abandon their young children – or use them as life's latest accessories, playthings to display? Do you revere youths who torture geese and goats for the sheer fun – or mock and mug passers-by?

What sort of person do *you* want to be? What sort of people would you like your children to become – or your parents to be or have been? Different answers may be offered; but almost certainly you would not be keen on those who are keen on the raping and pillaging, the torturing and mugging. You probably want friends and family to be happy, prosperous, healthy, contented. Perhaps specific features come to mind: being popular, having children – or a yacht – excelling at tennis, or taking up the flute with unbridled enthusiasm. Those are the sorts of things you may also want for yourself. You want to be happy – and that happiness typically involves knowing certain others are also happy.

The above considerations form the grounding of virtue ethics. People have recognizable reasons for doing what is right because doing what is right, it is argued, is likely to lead to their happiness. Morality and personal happiness are entwined. A consequentialist dimension is present, but one distant from the utilitarian's greatest happiness of the greatest number. Further, the happiness here is not understood solely as pleasure – or as constituted by owning a couple of yachts or delighting in a large share portfolio.

Happiness, flourishing and the virtues

Everyone desires happiness, wrote Aristotle. Although true, it is wrong to infer that there is a single happy state that all desire. Traditionally, every girl loves a sailor, but there is not one lucky sailor loved by every girl. It may, though, be argued that there are at least some common features necessary for the happiness that we all desire – basic good health, for instance.

In speaking of desiring happiness, we are not challenging the common observation – from philosophers to therapists to gurus – that if you deliberately seek happiness you are unlikely to find it. 'Ask yourself whether you are happy,' noted Mill, 'and you cease to be so.' We need to aim at things we value: piano-playing, weaving, reading the whole of Proust, cooking for friends. In aiming, even if not achieving, we may be happy – as later discovered, when looking back. There are nuances: we sometimes feel happier at the expectation of achievements than at the achievements; 'tis better to travel than to arrive. We sometimes place more value on possessing desires than on their satisfaction or quelling; witness some instances of sexual desire. We may prefer certain desires not to arise; witness again some sexual desires or those yearnings for yet more chocolates.

If you think you are happy, you are happy. Is that true? It is true that if you think you are having pleasures, then pleasures you are having; if you think you are in pain, then in pain you are. The happiness at work here – by Socrates, Plato and Aristotle, possibly Mill – lacks that self-certifying feature. Thinking that you are healthy does not certify health; you may unknowingly be seriously ill. The Greek concept is *eudaimonia*, rightly translated as happiness; but, to avoid misunderstanding, other translations are common: prosperity, flourishing, well-being, living well. Let us opt in the main for flourishing and living well; those states do not amount simply to having pleasures or material prosperity. Further, we may be mistaken about such states. Consider: Horatio's 'friends' are betraying him, yet he never finds out; he may think things are going well for him, but they are not at all.

Utilitarianism and deontological approaches focus on which actions are right; virtue ethics, it is casually said, focuses on what sort of person to be. Virtue ethics attends to agent centrality, as met within 'Jim and the Indians' (p. 36). This approach to ethics is offered in different flavours. A favoured flavour is Aristotle's; indeed, virtue ethics is sometimes deemed Aristotelianism or, more accurately, neo-Aristotelianism. The 'neo' registers revisions that depart from Aristotle's sidelining of women, slaves and barbarians.

Contrasting with Kant's starting point, virtue ethics starts with human biology: we – biological blobs – typically desire happiness; we desire to flourish. That makes the enterprise sound self-centred, even blatantly selfish. Virtue ethicists, as we shall see, reject that accusation.

The virtues of virtue ethics are not necessarily virtues whereby, historically, virtuous women were chaste. Virtues here are certain human excellences ('arête' is the Greek term). Aristotle saw them as excellences in performing our distinctive function as humans: the 'activity of the soul in accordance with reason' – that is, the truly good life is one of intellectual contemplation. Other times, Aristotle emphasized excellence in a range of human activities. Let us, though, resist Aristotelian exegesis, focusing instead on excellences of character – virtues – as understood by today's typical virtue ethicists. That is no immediate commitment to the classical cardinal virtues of temperance, prudence, courage and justice – or Christianity's faith, hope and charity. We hunt for deep character traits that engender our flourishing, our living well; those traits are, by definition, the virtues.

What ought you to do to secure health? If avoiding lung cancer is important – outweighing smoking's calming effects – then it is wise not to smoke. Smoking does not guarantee lung cancer; not smoking does not prevent lung cancer. We are judging likelihoods. Analogously, for many virtue ethicists virtue possession is neither sufficient nor necessary for a life to flourish – we may hit misfortunes or hit lucky – but being virtuous increases flourishing's likelihood.

For some virtue ethicists, in contrast, the virtues are necessary for flourishing, and even, argued Socrates and Plato, also sufficient: virtue is 'its own reward'. Dishonesty, for example, corrupts our living well, even if no one discovers our dishonesty and even if we glow within. After all, would you prefer success resulting from dishonesty and ruthlessness or from honesty and kindness? That is no knock-down question, and this is no place to engage Plato's detailed argument; so, we shall use the weasel words of 'involve' and 'contribute', leaving the exact linkage between virtues and the flourishing life in abeyance. Perhaps it just has to be accepted that some people can be horrible, vicious and uncaring, yet, in some sense, still flourish; perhaps it is wishful thinking to insist otherwise or to define 'flourishing' to rule out such possibilities.

Let us see how things work with a traditionally proclaimed virtue: honesty. Is honesty likely to contribute to living well? If you are honest, people will tend to trust you – and they, in return, are likely to be honest with you. If you are dishonest, people may find you out and steer clear; you may also feel bad about yourself. If people discover you to be honest solely because you want reciprocation, they may not be so well-disposed. Your honesty needs to involve telling others the truth for their sake. Thus it is that virtue ethicists attempt to rebuff the charge of coarse self-interest. Honesty, understood properly, is the best policy. Similar reasoning points to developing other virtues, such as courage, benevolence, temperance.

Being virtuous necessitates having certain emotions and

attitudes. That contrasts with Kant's insistence that moral motivation must be duty, not feelings. Consider jokes. Some grasp jokes
and cannot help but laugh; others need jokes explained, finally
comprehending, but without feeling the humour. Some others
do not get jokes at all; they are joke blind. Were Kant's approach
to morality applied here, he would value the middle group, those
who understand jokes, yet without emotion; virtue ethicists would
favour the first group, those with humour sensitivity. The third
group would be extreme amoralists, unable to 'get morality', unable
to 'get immorality'; they are outside the moral arena.

With the virtue ethicists' emphasis on right feelings, it is pretty
clear that people cannot just switch on the virtues. The virtues
have to be coaxed and developed; hence, there is a need, from
childhood, for moral training and education.

Swallows – and virtue as knowledge

One swallow does not make a spring. One act of generosity by
Scrooge does not make him generous. That comment, attributed
to Aristotle (well, the former comment), reminds us that character traits involve more than a few one-off actions. A night off
from painting – a drunken night – does not show that a man
is not a serious artist; a day off from morality does not make a
man a morally bad individual. A one-off case of abstinence from
'another drink' fails to show a man temperate; and you would
be unwise to rely on an individual solely on the basis of a single
act of generosity. Let us use courage – physical, intellectual and
emotional – to learn more about virtue.

Biological as we certainly are, we suffer pains – maybe medical
procedures, operations – and eventual demise. We need courage. We
may want to care for relatives in their last few days; think of the
regret if we let them down because queasy about dying. We need
courage. We are appalled at the gangs that threaten neighbours;

perhaps colleagues at work are being bullied by directors. Courage again is required, for we need to stand up and be counted. We made mistakes in advising customers; we could hide the mistakes. We need courage to own up. Cowards are rarely proud of their cowardice.

Some reasons for developing a character trait undermine that trait: courageous individuals fail to be truly courageous if the character trait was developed solely for achieving glory, promotion or a few medals. The right reason for acting courageously should not be that we want to behave courageously; that smacks of showing off. Courageous individuals act because they see that someone is in danger or a governmental wrongdoing should be exposed. Their motive is neither to appear courageous nor to chalk up possession of the virtue. They are not thinking of themselves.

Courageous individuals – also honest, kind and generous individuals – perform the required deeds willingly; they are pleased to do the right thing. Contrast with road-sweepers or teachers who sweep or teach very well, yet may well prefer a different occupation. The truly courageous do not wish that they lacked courage, thus avoiding the dangers into which their courage leads them.

Courageous individuals require sufficient perceptiveness and sensitivity to tell when 'brave' actions are appropriate – when whistle-blowing would help matters, when it would be wiser to adopt other tactics. Virtue failure – courage failure, here – may occur through ignorance of the facts. Hence, the intellectual virtues are important. Courageous individuals need 'practical wisdom'. He who leaps into a river to save some wailing children is not courageous if he cannot swim; his foolhardy 'hardy help' is likely to worsen the disaster. He shows fellow-feeling, not courage.

Such examples give weight to Aristotle's doctrine of the mean, whereby the virtue of courage lies between a cowardly disposition to run away and a foolish disposition to be reckless. In criticism, the doctrine lacks easy application to some virtues: what counts as the mean when it comes to honesty?

LIVING WELL:
BEYOND EXPERIENCES, BEYOND APPEARANCES

Betrayal – and not knowing: What constitutes the good life, living well, flourishing? The quick answer is happiness, prosperity, pleasures. On reflection, though, we may agree that even when people feel happy, prosperous and so forth, they may not be living well.

Suppose fidelity and family life are important to you, yet behind your back, your spouse and children betray you, speak badly of you. They stay with you because of your wealth and status. Even though you never find out, are you living well? Would we want to be so deceived?

Suppose on your death, people kick your corpse, tear up your will and mock your life's achievements. You know nothing about that, being deceased; but, did your life really go well?

Such questions at the very least suggest that there is more to living well than how you experience things in your lifetime.

Gyges' Ring: Plato, in *Republic*, refers to Gyges, a shepherd who found a ring which, when worn, made him invisible, enabling him to seduce the Queen and murder the King. Plato writes:

> Suppose two such magic rings, one given to the just man, the other to the unjust. No one, it is said, would stand fast in doing right, when he could go to the market and fearlessly help himself to anything he wanted, enter houses and sleep with any woman he chose.

Many people think that undetected wrongdoing can make them better off. Socrates and Plato reject that view. Truly good people would not succumb to wrongdoing, even with the Ring's protection. Wrongdoing would harm their integrity, their soul.

Suppose a good man unfairly suffers a very bad reputation, contrasting with a wicked man who, through deceit, is considered splendidly good. Which would you prefer to be? Plato answers, 'The good man.'

Goodness, not its appearance, says Plato, is essential to the flourishing life. On this view, the good individual cannot be harmed – even by betrayals such as those above – for goodness is a characteristic of the soul, immune to external vicissitudes. Apparently, the good man cannot be harmed, even if suffering on the rack.

Overall, virtue ethicists promote an ideal to which we should aspire, an ideal that, but for bad luck, should ensure a flourishing life. For the truly courageous – compassionate, honest – virtue should permeate their lives. The woman who rescues some children from a fire may be physically courageous, but cowardly when needing to confront emotional bullies at work. We can be, it seems, virtuous to greater or lesser degrees, more so in some areas than others – weak regarding passions of the flesh, strong regarding fighting injustice. Further, one virtue can surely be present without another. In Verdi's *Rigoletto*, Sparafucile, paid to murder, is outraged at the proposal that he could cheat his client by taking payment without delivering the goods, the corpse; he is no common thief but an honest man, pursuing his murdering trade. Further still, we may reasonably think that someone could live well without needing all the virtues. A country's leader may be courageous, admired, despite having no time for patience, pity or empathy. Socrates and Plato, though, arguing against those two 'further' thoughts, gave voice to the essential 'unity of the virtues'. Here is a way of unifying.

Courageous individuals need simple bravery, but also compassion, taking account of how their actions may risk harming others. The truly compassionate stand up courageously for the dispossessed. The courageous and compassionate must make honest appraisals of the circumstances. The honest person sometimes applies discretion. Kindness requires sensitivity to words: to the recently bereaved you may speak of the children having 'passed away', not of their being dead. The truly virtuous are good judges of what to say and when, of the morally salient. Similar considerations show that the virtuous need dispositions to be charitable, magnanimous and loyal – not selfish, arrogant, brutal. Thus, the virtues possess mutual dependency. Other desirable features of humans lack such linkages. We admire people who are polite and humorous. Someone, though, may be polite yet deadly serious; someone else witty yet rude.

Truly virtuous individuals possess the knowledge and wisdom of what is valuable in human life. Virtue failure may end up being understood as a failing in knowledge or a lack of wisdom. Those successfully employed, callously disparaging of the unemployed on social benefits, may be ignorant of unemployment's despairing hardships. Perhaps, though, they possess all the required factual knowledge, but are deficient in right feelings, in empathy. That deficiency may amount to ignorance; they do not know how to feel. Some people may yet possess the knowledge, the right feelings, but just cannot bring themselves, say, to write out the cheques to charity. They are weak-willed; their practical wisdom is impaired. (For weak will please see pp. 115–7.)

Doubting the virtue of virtue ethics

Is virtue ethics more successful in understanding morality than other attempts discussed so far? Virtue ethicists tend to ridicule rules and maxims propounded by utilitarians and deontologists; the good man does not rely on rules, but on his character, his wisdom. Virtue ethicists could, though, transform into virtue *theorists*, propounding rules to follow: be honest; be courageous; be compassionate. That to one side, not least because so many caveats would be required, virtue ethicists may rightly challenge other theorists by asking about motivations.

Whatever could motivate us to maximize overall happiness or to do something purely from Kantian duty? That is a good question, but do virtue ethicists fare much better in answering? Yes, when they stress personal happiness as the goal, our motivation is readily grasped; but when they present happiness as involving honesty, compassion, justice and so forth, for the sake of others – well, that we have motivations for happiness understood in that way is probably no more (or less) convincing than that we can be motivated by Kantian duty or the utilitarian goal.

Suppose we do value the Aristotelian virtues. We should still be baffled over what to do in particular circumstances. When is seeking to save the child foolhardy? When does empathy mean that we ought not to speak honestly? The general answer is: see what a wise and virtuous person does; but being unwise, deficient in virtue, how do I know – how can I even reasonably guess at – how a wise and virtuous agent would act?

Acquiring the virtues, comes the vague reply, takes time, with exposure to different circumstances, be they in reality, imagination or fiction. The Aristotelian emphasis on 'excellence' suggests analogies with practical skills. Consider the learning involved in becoming a skilful violinist, cook or craftsman in wood: it is by seeing how others perform and by developing sensitivities, imagination and judgement. The virtues can be acquired in a similar way. In the end, excellence in living does not mean working to a formula. Practical wisdom requires more – and less – than learning by rote.

The puzzle of what to do on particular occasions remains; but that fits the moral reality. Numerous moral dilemmas lack right answers of the form: *this* action must be performed rather than *that*. True, some theorists insist that there must always be a right answer, even if elusive; certainly any virtue ethicist of that ilk fails to tell us what is that answer in every case. We, the unwise, the unvirtuous, are usually told to judge, to weigh up factors – but how can we reach a well-judged decision when the values are incommensurable? There is, it seems, no distinctive 'right feature' to all right actions, a feature that just requires wider-awake eyes or stronger glasses.

An objection that strikes virtue ethics hard is summed up as 'cultural relativity'. Virtue ethicists make a virtue of deploying 'thick' moral concepts, such as courage, loyalty and decency, rather than the basic 'thin' concepts of right and wrong, good and bad. Different cultures, though, appear to promote different thick concepts; more accurately, concepts seemingly identical to ours are applied differently. Consider honour, disgrace and the role of blood money. What is honourable in one community is not so in another. Medieval Japanese culture possessed the concept of 'tsujigiri', meaning 'crossroads cut'. A warrior's samurai sword must slice in a single blow, if the warrior is not to be dishonoured in its ritual use. Consequently, a sword test was required. A way-farer – any unfortunate lowly person encountered – would be an accepted sword testing ground; could he be sliced with one blow?

South Africa's Afrikaners, before Nelson Mandela's presidency, could see themselves as flourishing, flourishing with Christian virtues; they virtually failed to recognize Asians and black Africans as human. In the US, it was not until 1964, with the growing Civil Rights movement, that racial segregation, with assumptions of white supremacy, was finally outlawed. In Aristotle's day, slavery was prominent and approved. Concern for slaves being good slaves was concern for their skill at slaving, not for what was good for them, for their sake, for their well-being.

Virtue ethicists of today may retort that such examples merely expose Aristotle's, the Afrikaners' and others' ignorance of common humanity. The truly virtuous possess the wisdom to see that respect for people cannot be restricted to 'our people'. The truly virtuous should also see that for people to live well they need a society where they have options and opportunities for, in Mill's terms, the higher pleasures; it is not enough to ensure that people have food and shelter, as if they flourish when grazing as mere animals.

Even if the truly virtuous grasp the above, flourishing may yet partly depend on society's ethos. In the West, and increasingly worldwide, values promoted by governments, corporations and the media are grounded in material prosperity, requiring home-ownership, a duty to consume, with frequent changes of phones, cars and fashions. We may challenge such values; but perhaps material prosperity is now at the heart of today's living well, affect-ing also, of course, what counts as happiness for utilitarians, even truthfulness for Kantian deontologists – think of political 'spin'.

In Britain, universities are increasingly business centres, expansion being necessary for flourishing. That is curious; some recent business models have led to global financial disasters, whereas, for decades, major British universities, promoting the ethos of research and academic excellence, not profits, were much envied. At a less elevated level, reflect how European football is dominated by transfer fees, glitz and some astonishing football salaries. Could someone today 'flourish' as a footballer, if excellent at the game, but receiving the national average income? Paradoxically, commercial success can occasionally devalue. Philip Glass is the most highly paid living composer, resulting, it seems, in some classical critics disparaging his work. Obviously, financial factors should impinge neither way on the music's musical value.

We need to turn to Socrates and Plato to secure an idea of flourishing without dependence on the community's ethos. They provide an inwardness, a certain solipsism to the good life, a solipsism in that the individual can flourish independently of the views of others, independently even of physical torments. The good man has harmony in his soul, control of his passions; he is psychologically healthy. For Plato, that health is mysteriously reached by opening eyes to the Good. Mystery apart, even harmony as essential to flourishing can be doubted. Perhaps some can flourish with internal conflicts or within diverse social worlds.

Questions of personal identity arise here: what constitutes the self as a unity, the soul as in harmony? More down to earth, we may note how Marx and Engels valued, not immaterial souls, but flesh-and-blood individuals, human beings, enjoying diversity: people would take advantage of opportunities 'to hunt in the morning, fish in the afternoon, rear cattle in the evening, criticise after dinner, without ever becoming hunter, fisherman, herdsman or critic'. That direction away from *being* a hunter or fisherman and so forth chimes, as we shall see in Chapter 6, with Sartre's repudiation of bad faith. How unified or fixed must, or can, the good life be? Is it, in fact, determined by biology?

MACHIAVELLI: VIRTUES AND FORTUNA

Learning how not to be good: Niccolò Machiavelli (1469–1527), a Florentine diplomat, is typically understood as machiavellian; yet there is more – and less – to Machiavelli than that. He writes:

> Many have dreamed up republics and principalities which have never in truth been known to exist; the gulf between how one should live and how one does live is so wide that a man who neglects what is actually done for what should be done moves towards self-destruction.

To maintain power, a prince must learn how not to be good; the aim is state security, bringing prosperity for citizens and honour for himself. Aristotle might have approved – so far.

The virtues: It is laudable, says Machiavelli, to possess the virtues, but leaders must also have regard for consequences:

> A prince must not worry if he incurs reproach for his cruelty so long as he keeps his subjects united and loyal. By making an example or two he will prove more compassionate than those who, being too compassionate, allow disorders leading to murder and rapine. These harm a community, but executions ordered by a prince affect only individuals.

Dirty hands? Machiavelli wanted Florence, state and citizens, to flourish. The citizens must uphold classical morality, keeping promises, and so on. The prince, though, addresses a bigger picture. He rightly lies and kills, when necessary for Florentine prosperity. What is right for him can be wrong for others because of the different roles. Recall Government House utilitarianism (p. 35), but without its cosmopolitan concern for the global community.

We can see how governments may rightly follow policies that individuals should resist: perhaps a government refuses to pay kidnappers to release victims – its duty is to discourage kidnapping – but the victims' friends, out of love and compassion, just have to try to raise the required funds.

Fortuna: Machiavelli, a realist, noted that success depended in part on luck, Fortuna – on, as British Prime Minister Harold Macmillan would say, 'Events, dear boy, events'. In Machiavelli's sexist mode, Fortuna is a woman; she favours young men's audacity over the elderly's obstinacy. She is fickle; political leaders, to achieve success, must be flexible.

Appealing (to) nature

Naturalistic ethics appeals to nature – to our biological constitution, to our being human – for determining what is good
and bad, right and wrong. Virtue ethics is hence 'naturalistic'.
Aristotle, drawing on how humans are constituted, tells of the
best life. Although he describes it as one of self-sufficiency, it is far
removed from the solitary, but is enmeshed in family, friends and
community; our human nature is that of political social beings.
Questions immediately arise. Is he right about the natural facts to
which he appeals? Even if he is, how does that show them – and
which ones – to be valuable? Even if some are valuable, maybe
we ought to go beyond them? Perhaps there is value in playing
draughts; but it should be more fulfilling to rise to chess. Of course,
biological facts rule out lots of activities. A morality that required
us to fly unaided would be deviant and pointless.

Aristotle was investigating over two thousand years before
Darwin. As with Kant centuries later, he saw worldly explanations
as partly teleological: items, if unforced, naturally behave as if with
ends 'being sought'. Contrasting with fire and air, stones and water
'by their nature' strive towards the Earth, their *telos* or end. Human
beings, by their nature, and other creatures, by their (different)
natures, possess distinctive functions; to flourish is to excel in what
is distinctive to the species. Although we largely lack Aristotle's
teleological eyes, his approach resonates regarding functions and
roles that we create. We grasp what it is for surgeons to be good
surgeons – that is, acting well in their function as surgeons. We
are using 'good' attributively: to tell whether something is a good
X, we need to know what it is for; the 'good' is not free-standing,
but tied to the 'X'.

Roles generate duties. Nurses and the police have duties of
care that differ from those of passers-by or teachers. Patience
and courage are needed, yet in different ways. Emphasizing
roles as requiring well-recognized virtues – compassion, honesty,

fairness – instead of stressing rule books and box-ticking exercises could possibly help reduce scandals of careless nursing and of sales targets outweighing customer concern. People who are good in their special functions and roles may not, of course, function as good people, excellent at being human – quite whatever it is that constitutes excellence in that functioning. Although today we standardly do not understand good human beings as good at their human functioning, recognizable obligations do arise from natural roles, such as those of parents to their children. We may go further: in virtue of being human, as citizens of the world – if we can make sense of that cosmopolitanism – we possess certain duties to help others.

Whatever it is to excel at a function or role – as sailor, shepherd or scoundrel – as mother, lover or world citizen – there remains the question of which functions, roles and institutions are morally desirable. We value doctors, teachers, farmers, cleaners and craftsmen; we may also recognize that a flourishing society needs poets, musicians, even philosophers. Controversy arises if we include courtesans, surrogacy agencies, royalty and lion-tamers. We may well have doubts about derivatives traders, astrologers and Masters of the Hounds; and it is difficult to see how a morality can approve of 'cutters' who perform female genital mutilation and harems that demand eunuchs.

When virtue ethicists appeal to the natural, it may be to *values* that we naturally as humans hold, 'natural' being here a moralized concept. Our practices show that we naturally possess feelings for others, enjoy friendships – and evaluate them as good. Aristotle observed that an individual would not choose to have all the good things by himself – well, he forgot about hermits – but he is right for the most part.

On arrival in faraway lands, Aristotle noted, we encounter human communities that usually recognize travellers and their needs. We can, of course, dream up creatures, human-like save for the virtues. Odysseus encountered the Cyclopes: they lacked extensive fellow-feeling; they would eat the guests invited to their dinner table. Cyclopes were unyoked from society, bereft of human nature, and hence of morality. Atrocities committed in war and civil unrest should remind us, though, how humans can readily, so readily, become Cyclopic; but in the main, we should agree – even the warring perpetrators should agree – that, when engaged in horrendous acts of strife and brutality, humanity scarcely flourishes.

Emphasis on our natural beliefs and feelings, as the way into morality, has the advantage of ready recognition of, and feeling for, the morality derived; it has the disadvantage that morality may collapse into majority opinion. Reflect on the oppression in many societies of homosexual activities because 'unnatural'. How one determines what is natural raises many puzzles, but, in any case, no reliable connection exists between something's naturalness and its being right. Your natural hair colour may not be right for you; his natural desire for revenge may be morally wrong.

Entering morality via *human* flourishing also merits criticism: why, morally, should humanity take top priority in determining the good? Many goods are not goods because they contribute to human flourishing – if they contribute at all. Securing the truth is a good – and would be so, even if of no aid to human flourishing. The well-being of badgers is a good, yet without any obvious contribution to human flourishing. Presumably, according to religions, God is an exceptional good – Goodness itself – yet not because of humanity's well-being.

♈

The theories so far discussed present some practical overlap, but also much conflict. Deliverances from Kant's Categorical Imperative conflict with utilitarians' greatest happiness and with virtue ethicists' emphasis on right feelings; virtue ethicists have little regard for utilitarian and Kantian universality and impartiality.

Our medley on morality has displayed some unease with all the theories. Suppose you come to the rescue of the distressed; is the right tone struck if you explain that your reason, your motivation, was to be virtuous or to do your moral duty, or to maximize happiness? Our medley has, though, found value in all the theories for highlighting typical, though different, moral concerns – concerns for human welfare, happiness, respect for individuals; in some areas, impartiality and universality; in other areas, partialities and agent centrality. Most people, most societies, recognize values of honesty, generosity and fairness – and the frequent difficulties in determining their correct application.

Regarding that motley cargo – that cargo labelled 'morality' – is there any way God can help?

5

God: dead or alive?

People often ask, 'Whence does morality derive?' 'God' is the answer on the lips of many. Rabbis, bishops and imams insist religion and ethics are essentially entwined. That insistence receives support well beyond religious authority. Many people, even the non-religious – from politicians to pundits to publicans – casually assume that religion and morality are linked. In contrast, slogans from atheistic humanists emphasize how we can be good without God; a slogan, of course, is no argument, no argument at all.

Earlier chapters have shown the absence of consensus on morality's grounding and its particular demands. Do appeals to religious belief help resolve the difficulties?

We need to distinguish between the following positions: that morality requires the existence of God; that morality requires belief in God; and that morality requires both. Further puzzles arise: must believers be motivated by the divine will in order to act morally? Need believers of different faiths maintain that they all worship one and the same divinity? Should religion, in the end, amount to no more than 'to do good', as Thomas Paine described his religion?

Putting the further puzzles to one side, let us focus on some possible links between religion and morality. Here is one possibility: perhaps moral truths depend upon God, but people fail to believe that they do. Suppose everyone is atheist. They may still observe moral rules valuing life, liberty and fairness – perhaps because they understand those rules and moral motivations as aiding social harmony. That scenario is certainly possible. The people have just made a mistake over morality's grounds; God constitutes the grounds.

Here is another, very different, possibility: suppose we – everyone, even – believe sincerely in God's existence. That *belief* may be necessary, even sufficient grounds for moral behaviour; yet the belief in God, in a divine lawgiver, is false. Here is a modification to that possibility: perhaps religious authorities know that God is a myth, yet encourage religious practices to shore up people's moral commitment. That modified possibility may be likened to Government House utilitarianism, where only those in the moral know, know – though those authorities at least possess utilitarian justification for the deceit. If authorities wittingly encourage mistaken belief in God, they may have any manner of motivation, perhaps the maintenance of power and prestige. Or, perhaps religion arises as solace, given the world's material conditions – in Marx's terms:

> Religion is the sigh of the oppressed creature, the heart of a heartless world, just as it is the spirit of a spiritless situation. It is the opium of the people.

On this view, religion provides an illusory happiness; alterations to our material conditions are necessary for true happiness.

Whence derives morality?

The existence of mathematical and logical truths, of abstract entities such as numbers, fails to tease atheists from atheism; but morality's existence leads some atheistically inclined to yield up their atheism. Moral properties, it is argued, cannot emerge from the physical world, but can derive from a non-physical divinity. Morality goes along with obligations from conscience, feelings of duty, sufferings from guilt; they surely, it is said, arise only because of powerful divine demands. Of course, we ought not to rely on deliverances of (seeming) conscience just because they are of such; conscience can lead to horrendous outcomes – think of the sometimes horrendous treatment of heretics and apostates. Adolf Eichmann, on trial for Nazi war crimes, declared that he would have had a bad conscience had he not obeyed orders.

God arrives in moral thinking via two distinct lines. One line, as just noted, takes us from morality's existence to belief in God. A second line has God's existence and nature settled in advance of moral considerations. That settlement results from scripture, revelation or non-moral arguments. From that settlement, morality is deduced as flowing from God. Non-moral arguments include design arguments whence the world's orderliness or complexity points to a divine designer and creator. A variant design argument emphasizes the apparent vast improbability of a universe existing with conscious rational creatures – unless through divine intent. The arguments are open to many challenges, and not just from atheists. Atheist humanists could argue that if God exists, granting us reason, then to respect him, we ought paradoxically not to believe in him, for the arguments to his existence are so poor. Hereafter, we use 'humanist' to cover those who do not believe in God, yet who believe in moral values; they are not nihilists.

Belief in God is often a faith rather than conclusion of formal arguments. Faith in God is not usually treated as akin to belief in a special grandiose empirical item; it is more a commitment to an external grounding for the universe, radically different from worldly items, yet still appropriately described as 'loving' and 'good', 'creator of man in his own image'. God is usually taken as omnipotent (all powerful), omniscient (all knowing) and omnibenevolent (all good and caring for humanity). He is often conceived as omnipresent, yet also eternal and outside of time.

However God arrives on the scene, he is lawgiver. Moral laws – any laws – require an appropriate authority. The moral lawgiver cannot be another human being, the government or the state's

SPINOZA: THE GOD-INTOXICATED ATHEIST?

Baruch Spinoza (1632–77), a Portuguese Jew, born in Amsterdam, became a fine lens-grinder after trouble with his synagogue. He declined professorships, but was sought after by notable philosophers for his views – and lenses. Spinoza was ascetic, save for pipe-smoking, wine and casting flies into spiders' webs, laughing at ensuing battles.

'A book forged in hell' was an accolade Spinoza's *Treatise* received for defending free speech and toleration. His *Ethics*, a masterpiece published posthumously, reaped similar condemnation for arguing that 'God' and 'Nature' denote the same one substance, and that nature is not designed with hidden purposes. Explanations ending with refuge in God's will manifest 'the sanctuary of ignorance'. Blessedness, love of God, amounts to our understanding natural causes, thus attaining peace of mind.

His apparent pantheism led some to deem him God-intoxicated – God is everywhere – others saw him as atheist: God is just the natural world, viewed in a certain way. He was revered by many, from Goethe to Einstein, for his integrity, humility and rationality.

Excommunication: Spinoza, from youth, questioned Judaism's claims. In 1656, his Amsterdam synagogue excommunicated him:

> Cursed be he by day, and cursed be he by night; cursed be he when he lieth down, and cursed be he when he riseth up; cursed be he when he goeth out and cursed be he when he cometh in; the Lord will not pardon him; the wrath and fury of the Lord will be kindled against this man, and bring down upon him all the curses which are written in the Book of the Law; and the Lord will destroy his name from under the heavens; and, to his undoing, the Lord will cut him off from all the tribes of Israel, with all the curses of the firmament which are written in the Book of the Law…

This may remind us how intolerant religions can be – yet also how they can change for the good. Today's Judaic authorities may lift his excommunication. One must not be hasty.

courts. Your parents may tell you not to break promises, but that they tell you is not what makes promise-breaking wrong. That the government prohibits drug use is not what makes it morally wrong (if it is). Only a divine lawgiver, a moral commander, can account for the force of moral duty, of conscience. Sometimes a further moral argument is presented, namely, that God must exist, otherwise there could be no guarantee of ultimate justice, no guarantee that people's eventual happiness will be proportionate to their moral worthiness. Of course, we may question the belief that there must be such guarantees.

The natural law: declarations and scripture

Morality as essentially grounded in natural law, divinely determined, is the typical religious understanding, though many natural law theorists these days dispense with the divinity, arguing that there just are some goods in nature, some natural goods, such as possession of the truth, deep personal relationships, even play; we should pursue them and respect them. Some humanists could endorse that position.

Natural law, divinely grounded, is most famously associated with St Thomas Aquinas, but it is also found in Aristotle and earlier. The thought is that, just as there are laws of nature, of how things *do* behave – accounting for planetary movements, expansion of gases and so forth – so there are moral laws built within nature directing how human beings *ought* to behave. Here is John Locke, seventeenth-century philosopher:

> The state of nature has a law of nature to govern it, which obliges every one: and reason, which is that law, teaches all mankind, who will but consult it, that being all equal and independent, no one ought to harm another in his life, health, liberty, or possessions.

Locke grounds the above in his conviction that men are 'the workmanship of one omnipotent, and infinitely wise maker'. He infers that 'when his own preservation comes not in competition' man ought, as much as he can, to:

> preserve the rest of mankind, and may not, unless it be to do justice on an offender, take away, or impair the life, or what tends to the preservation of the life, the liberty, health, limb, or goods of another.

The 1776 American *Declaration of Independence*, drafted by Thomas Jefferson after joint discussions, was probably influenced by Locke's thinking. It speaks of the Creator endowing men with 'certain unalienable Rights' among which are 'Life, Liberty and the pursuit of Happiness'. Natural law, as in that Declaration, is commanded by God, a divine gift. In France's 1789 *Declaration of the Rights of Man and the Citizen*, there is cursory reference to man's rights being under the auspices of the Supreme Being.

Despite the declarations' worthy words, implying divine support, the American Congress ensured elimination of reference to slavery, thereby also ensuring that slavery itself would *not* be eliminated; and France's National Convention's members proclaimed their benevolence. About the members, Chateaubriand noted, 'these devotees of philanthropy had their neighbours beheaded for the sake of the greatest happiness of the human race.' Morally, on the divine natural law theory, we must follow God's laws, but how can we tell what those laws amount to – to slaves lacking the rights of others; to beheadings being permissible?

Locke relies on reason; others proclaim moral insight, scriptural persuasion or our sense of humanity. In theory, utilitarianism could hence possess natural law backing. Bentham, as noted, spoke of natural rights – of natural law – as nonsense on stilts, but the natural law, divinely determined, could indeed be to maximize happiness; but for what divine purpose?

What are the underlying duties, the moral contents, set by God? Some believe they must be to act in our own self-interest, that self-interest including concern for parents, children and lovers. Hobbes speaks of reason showing the first law of nature to be: 'seek peace and follow it', the second law being the right of nature: 'by all means we can to defend ourselves'. We may again wonder how such rights are revealed by reason, just as we may question the religious reliance on certain selected texts – 'the scriptures' – with certain preferred interpretations or within approved traditions. The dubiety of such reliance is insurmountable for non-believers, but, for believers, faith enables surmounting.

One problem is that ancient scripture, even one particular text, contains factual falsehoods. There are inconsistent biblical accounts of creation and of Jesus' life; add in the Qur'an and other scriptures, and we have a mishmash of tales, taking us from the Red Sea being parted to God making a mortal virgin pregnant – to the existence of mixed angels. Minimally, inconsistencies show that scripture cannot always be factually reliable. Careful interpretations may not help: some creationists believe the universe was created around six thousand years ago – Earth is young – while others follow current cosmology, the universe being billions of years old, though still divinely created with a purpose.

Factual unreliability need not undermine scripture's moral value. As Cardinal Baronius wrote, the Bible tells us not how the heavens go, but how to go to Heaven. Scripture offers a valuable and consistent moral code – yet is that true? Texts differ and scholarly interpretations vie with scholarly interpretations over morality relating to sexual relations, slavery, our use of the Earth, and the treatment of non-believers on Earth and in eternity. There can hence be no pure reliance on the texts. The different textural renderings probably indicate the believers' pre-existing moral sense rather than a divine morality bursting from the pages. Of course, that pre-existing moral sense may yet be divinely inspired.

Believers may determine what is right as that which would

be to God's glory; the questions then become: what is that glory and how is it morally relevant?

True, religious texts provide some appealing injunctions, notably ones that amount to, 'do unto others as you would have them do unto you'. The injunctions, though, are original to neither the Bible nor the Qur'an; and they are not the preserve of the religious. That apart, they still need justification or explanation. How should we interpret the 'do unto others' injunction? Maybe I would like to live in a peaceful mansion with servants and concubines – so must I provide that for others? Perhaps because that is what I should have to provide, I need to quell such grandee desires. If so, it would also transpire that I ought not to want others to engage in life-saving surgery on me, if I do not want to engage similarly on them (given my lack of medical skills). Even with the popular 'do unto others', work is thus required to grasp what nuanced version is morally justified.

Injunctions such as 'do not kill' are not suddenly easily applied because divinely grounded; believers are as muddled as non-believers regarding when a war is just, when killing civilians is proportionate and whether refraining from killing is wrong if sufferers need help to die. Additionally, scriptural commands gleaned and interpreted still raise the question of whether, morally, they should receive our obedience, our blessing. If the commands are ultimately derived from God, an all-good, loving being – not merely from some ancient authors – then that should carry weight. It should carry weight until we reflect further on the characteristics of God. We shall now reflect.

Divine commands, *Euthyphro* and regress

Doing your duty, through divine commands, is to be obeying orders. If being good and doing the right thing means obeying someone else's commands, then the commander can himself only be good if also obeying external commands. We run into a regress: God would need further authorities over him. For regressive avoidance, morality must not have ultimate grounds in obedience to independent commanders: God must possess moral characteristics in want of no further authority. How, though, is it known that he does possess such characteristics – and what makes them *moral* characteristics? Furthermore, why is morality seen as needing an external lawgiver when, finally, a moral rabbit is pulled from a divine hat, a rabbit in no need of an external anything?

We are approaching a much-discussed dilemma, the *Euthyphro* dilemma, derived from a conversation between Euthyphro and Socrates in the eponymously titled dialogue by Plato. The dialogue's dilemma addresses piety and what is God-beloved; in current discussions, the dilemma focuses on the good and divine commands.

> Is something good purely because God commands it or does God command something purely because it is good?

Which way should we go? A similar dilemma lurked in virtue ethics: is something good because it contributes to human flourishing, or does something contribute to human flourishing because it is good? With divinity to hand, let us muse upon each of the dilemma's horns.

The first horn is that what is good is determined by whatever it is God commands – be it by definition or other linkage. Goodness cannot, though, be *defined* as what God commands; it is a significant question whether goodness is what God commands. If God were to command the killing of first-born children, that would surely not make the killing morally right or the outcome good. The response can be that God would not command such things; it is a pity, though, that some believe that God did issue such a command regarding the first-born of Egypt (see *Exodus* 13:15) and is the cause of other horrors.

Many believers insist that God would not really command horrendous things; the ancient texts need interpretation. Insistence on interpretation again suggests that we possess a moral sense independently of God's commands. Further, on this horn of the dilemma, if we have no sense of the right and the good independently of what God commands, then to praise God as all good is to praise him for commanding whatever he chooses to command. Furthermore, God's motivation towards goodness is but a motivation to do anything he decides; on what basis does he decide? Overall, we should reject the dilemma's horn whereby the right and good are right and good purely because God says so.

The dilemma's second horn is that God commands certain things because they are right or good; they are not right or good because God so commands. That suggests that goodness is external to God and his commands. In landing on this horn, we are accepting, it seems, the possibility that we humans could have access to what is right and good without reference to God. On the surface, that should be a happy landing. Falling onto the second horn is unwanted only for those committed to morality being essentially constituted by God and his ways.

We need, though, to take our time. The considerations posed by the dilemma's horns are not as clear as the above conveys. Perhaps goodness can be understood independently of God, yet still necessarily depend upon God. For an analogy, consider the concept of a right angle: it is a necessary feature of a square, yet can be understood independently of the concept of a square.

One intriguing proposal is that God and goodness are identical. In praising God for his goodness, we are simply valuing goodness. For the religious, though, duty, conscience and moral law imply a personal authority, a creator. How is such an authority possible, if the authority is goodness, and not person-like at all? There are attempted answers: maybe our talk of God is our stumbling to see that an ethical requirement – Goodness itself – possesses creative powers, creating the universe which is unfolding towards itself, towards Goodness. Even if that idea makes sense – and we may have serious doubts – it does not follow that it is true.

Motivations, right reasons – and Pascal's Wager

'Give your evidence,' said the King, 'and don't be nervous or I'll have you executed on the spot.'

That line from Lewis Carroll's *Alice's Adventures in Wonderland* shows how what is said can undermine what is sought through what is said; the witness quakes all the more, given the King's words. In the BBC's *Dad's Army*, the Captain, telling Private Pike not to disclose his name to the enemy, says, in front of the enemy, 'Don't tell them your name, Pike!' Analogously, if morality requires doing as God commands and such doings – as many maintain – aid the likelihood of eternal bliss, then believing in that bliss may undermine the doers' moral worthiness. Why?

Morally praiseworthy actions are performed for right reasons; yet those reasons could be quashed, if the aim, through pleasing God, is our own heavenly outcome. Many religious authorities resist offering possibilities of personal eternal life; but undoubtedly numerous believers act 'because that is what the Bible or the Qur'an says, and is the way to heaven'. The promise of eternal bliss apparently leads some into martyrdom, killing themselves as well as others. Moral behaviour here is nothing more than simple long-term self-interest, be it for eternal bliss or avoidance of eternal damnation.

A related problem arises with the famous Pascal's Wager. Pascal, a deeply religious seventeenth-century mathematician and philosopher, argued that because of the risk of eternal damnation, compared with the lesser inconveniences of worship and confession, it is prudent to believe in God 'just in case'. The probability calculations are open to question; should you manifest your belief in God by church attendance – synagogue or mosque? Should you be of the Judaic or Muslim faith? Maybe worshipping the wrong god, or the one God in the wrong way, has worse consequences than worshipping none at all.

Ignoring the calculation, how can we come to believe sincerely in God? We cannot switch on genuine beliefs at will. We cannot believe that God exists or that whatever God tells us is morally right, 'just like that'. Of course, we may hope that engaging in religious rituals – wanting to believe – is good enough for God. Perhaps being surrounded by godly believers could even lead to genuine belief; perhaps belief is contagious. A second difficulty arises. The self-interested motivation in seeking belief in God could tarnish any belief acquired, preventing us from being true believers in the sight of God.

Even if the religious are not motivated by self-interest – even if conversion motivations do not undermine belief – God's role can sometimes be used, or misused, throwing the morality of the behaviour into doubt. Here are two throws.

First, when religious believers defend their behaviour as moral, their defence can amount to passing the moral buck, relying on the 'moral testimony' of others, notably God: 'I am behaving thus because God commands me'; 'I do this because the Qur'an tells me so'. *Moral* reasons for moral actions should be of the order 'because the actions are right, or fair, or to prevent those people from suffering'. A well-known, non-religious manifestation of dubious buck-passing is that of combatants, defending their morally questionable actions by announcing that they were 'just doing their duty, following orders'.

Secondly, when the 'I defer to authority' stance is to an authority taken as omnipotent, demanding complete obedience, it is understandable that the deferrer would not dare challenge

FROM NATURE TO… GOD'S GOODNESS?

Benjamin Franklin (1706–90), 'The First American' – though his only remaining home is now a museum in London – wrote:

> Behold the rain which descends from heaven upon our vineyards, there it enters the roots of the vines, to turn into wine, a constant proof that God loves us, and loves to see us happy.

Giacomo Leopardi (1798–1837), of *The Leopard*, noted in *Zibaldone*:

> Go into a garden of plants, grass, flowers. No matter how lovely it seems… you will be unable to look anywhere and not find suffering. Here a rose is attacked by the sun, which has given it life; it withers, languishes, wilts… That tree is infested by an ant colony, that other one by caterpillars, flies, snails, mosquitoes… The spectacle of such abundance of life when you first enter this garden lifts your spirits… But in truth this life is wretched and unhappy, every garden is like a vast hospital…

Charles Darwin (1809–82) lost his Christian faith, it seems, mainly because of his daughter Annie's suffering and death, rather than his evolutionary theory. In his *Autobiography* we find:

> That there is much suffering in the world no one disputes. Some have attempted to explain this in reference to man by imagining that it serves for his moral improvement. But the number of men in the world is as nothing compared with that of all other sentient beings and these often suffer greatly without any moral improvement.

Arthur Schopenhauer (1788–1860), philosopher of pessimism, in his *On the Suffering of the World*, rejects God because of:

> the misery which abounds everywhere; and the obvious imperfection of its highest product, man, who is a burlesque of what he should be…
> The conviction that the world and man is better not to have been, is of a kind to fill us with indulgence towards one another. We might well consider the proper form of address to be, not Monsieur, Sir, mein Herr, but my fellow-sufferer… It reminds us of that which is the most necessary thing in life – the tolerance, patience, regard, and love of neighbour of which everyone stands in need, and which every man owes to his fellow.

that authority. Appeals to any authority have dangers – they may be just excuses – but the danger here flows from the authority's assumed omnipotence; it takes priority over natural compassion and fellow-feeling. Think of Abraham's preparedness to sacrifice his son; think of horrendous deeds performed supposedly in the name of Allah. Think, indeed, of horrendous deeds performed because of oppressive God-like secular authorities such as the one-time Soviet state or the powerful appeal to many of patriotism, of 'The Flag'.

The problem of evil

With God and goodness held as entwined, an outstanding problem comes to the fore, that of the immensity of worldly sufferings, of extreme despairs, terrors and helplessness. It is the Problem of Evil. God, as said, is usually understood as omnipotent, omniscient and omnibenevolent. In this world, though, there are considerable (seemingly) unnecessary sufferings, taken as evils, gratuitous evils. People suffer natural evils through earthquakes, volcanoes and other environmental events; there are pains of dental decay, ageing and seeing loved ones suffering and dying. As Mill noted regarding the animal kingdom:

> If a tenth part of the pains which have been expended in finding benevolent adaptations in all nature, had been employed in collecting evidence: to blacken the character of the Creator, what scope for comment would not have been found in the entire existence of the lower animals, divided, with scarcely an exception, into devourers and devoured, and a prey to a thousand ills from which they are denied the faculties necessary for protecting themselves!

Additional to natural evils are moral evils. Millions suffer moral evils – evils caused by humans deliberately inflicting harms. Witness the numerous tortures and bombings of civilians in war-torn lands. On a smaller scale, reflect on the unkindnesses we can perpetrate, ignoring people in distress, passing thoughtless comments or lacking generosity of spirit.

Natural and moral evils sometimes combine. Some people are naturally callous and cannot help being so; others may deliberately choose to spread natural diseases, causing immense suffering.

Regarding any and all evils, why does God tolerate them? God could surely have prevented them; that he has not proves that either God is not omnipotent or does not care. Perhaps he lacks omnipotence; perhaps his omniscience does not cover future events. Maybe he lacks care about worldly sufferings, but then he cannot be omnibenevolent; he cannot be morality's lawgiver. The world's sufferings thus form a springboard for humanist arguments that God as typically understood in Judaism, Christianity and Islam, cannot exist. In believing that God exists, believers are placing God's nature in a poor light, given the world's miseries. Simone Weil, deeply religious – even something of a religious mystic – recognizes evil's disturbance:

> There is only one time when I really know nothing of this certitude of God's love any longer. It is when I am in contact with the affliction of other people, those who are indifferent or unknown to me as much as the others, perhaps even more, including those of the most remote ages of antiquity. This contact causes me such atrocious pain and so utterly rends my soul that as a result the love of God becomes almost impossible for a while. It would take very little more to make me say impossible – so much so that I am uneasy about myself.

Weil reassures herself of God's love 'by remembering that Christ wept on foreseeing the horrors of the destruction of Jerusalem'. She hopes that God will forgive her for her compassion. That, to non-believers, illustrates a danger of belief in divine authority: astonishingly, one may feel bad about one's compassion.

Life would be bland and boring – unrecognizable as human – were there neither struggles in securing achievements nor failures to be met. There are, though, as briefly listed, many sufferings, pains, distresses that appear highly unwarranted and not at all essential to human lives securing fulfilment; indeed, just the opposite is the case. Some distresses, apparently, result expressly from divine deliberation: for example, God's treatment of his servant Job, raining down immense sufferings. The Paradox of Job highlights the existence of sufferings undeservedly placed on humans.

One overall response, designed to uphold God with traditional 'omni' features, is that what seems gratuitous evil is not really so. The nineteenth-century philosopher Brentano, for example, welcomed his blindness; it prevented him from distractions that would have impeded his work. Evils would be correctly seen not as evils, were we possessed of the divine perspective of eternity; we need sight of the bigger picture. That wildly optimistic stance could receive a wildly pessimistic alternative; perhaps what appears good is not really good – the world is the work of the Devil, once seen from the correct perspective. Were we initially neutral about the nature of any divine designer, the evidence would surely point as much to an evil power as to one of good will.

How may these various problems associated with evil be handled by those who judge morality to be grounded in a supremely good divinity? We humans permit numerous evils and sufferings through ignorance, weakness or nastiness; God, it is believed, lacks such features. God is often said to be Love and Reason.

Some maintain God's goodness, arguing that without sufferings, there could be no exercise of certain virtues. God must permit some evils – for the greater good of people manifesting compassion and benevolence. The world is a moral training ground, a 'vale of Soul-making' to use Keats' expression. A quick response is that sufferers would probably prefer to forgo the compassion and settle for no suffering in the first place. It is curious that a just God would be so calculating – to make millions of innocent people suffer, so that some others may practise compassion. That is treating the sufferers as means to an end; it hardly respects them.

God, however powerful, cannot do the logically impossible. He cannot create a round square or an immovable boulder; there cannot be compassion without suffering. Maybe for goodness to exist there must be some evil; just as for tallness, there must be shortness. The wise reply is that even were goodness relativistic in that way – a concession open to doubt – that would leave the vast quantity of evils, of sufferings, unexplained. There is a nuanced supplement. Suppose goodness logically requires evil to exist: then, if it is possible for God not to have created a world – as some claim – in such circumstances God could not be good, for there would be no evils. That is a puzzle over God's own goodness.

Sometimes it is argued that for humans to be aware of the good/evil distinction, good and evil must both exist. Even were that so, may we not learn the distinction through fiction? In any case, the consideration again fails to justify the quantity of evil: presumably, one speck of known evil would suffice.

Being essentially omnipotent and omnibenevolent, God must have created the best of all possible worlds – thus argued the eminent philosopher and mathematician Gottfried Wilhelm Leibniz, duly ridiculed in Voltaire's *Candide*. Perhaps there exist goods unknown to humans, goods that logically require the evils only too well known. Because no known goods, such as compassion, can justify the amount of suffering, it does not follow that no unknown goods can. Perhaps some evils are necessary to a universe. Those approaches presuppose a loving, omnipotent deity; but again, what justifies that presupposition? That question to one side, explanations of the surrounding evil are but appeals to the mystery of unknowns. Mystery is no good answer to a puzzle, but a puzzling repetition of puzzlement.

HOW TO VIEW THE WORLD: THE GARDEN

The gardener: Today's scientists do not seek purposes or designs to explain the natural world; the religious do. Here is John Wisdom's 1944 tale:

> Two people return to their long-neglected garden and find among the weeds a few of the old plants surprisingly vigorous. One says, 'It must be that a gardener has been coming and doing something about these plants.' Upon enquiry they find that no neighbour has ever seen anyone in their garden. The first man says, 'He must have worked while people slept.' The other says, 'No… anybody who cared about the plants would have kept down these weeds.' The first man says, 'Look at the way these are arranged. There is purpose and a feeling for beauty here. I believe that someone comes, someone invisible to mortal eyes… the more carefully we look the more we shall find confirmation of this.'

Religious rituals – on the Sabbath – can offer the world anew, a whole, an eternity. The rabbi says, 'In the Torah there is no before and after.' The religious impulse presents the world as a gift. It is more than a mechanical system of causes and effects; it merits piety and awe. Compare with paintings and music. Chemists may explain the pigments and physicists the air vibrations; but those explanations say nothing about the picture's representation, the music's melody and beauty. Science does not have the last word.

Wittgenstein (1889–51) showed the importance of what cannot be said:

> I was walking about in Cambridge and passed a bookshop, and in the window were portraits of Russell, Freud and Einstein. A little further on, in a music shop, I saw portraits of Beethoven, Schubert and Chopin. Comparing these portraits I felt intensely the terrible degeneration that had come over the human spirit in the course of only a hundred years.

There is more to understanding life and the world than analysis and grasp of nature's laws. Wise individuals, the mystics who find sense in life, notes Wittgenstein, are unable to say in what that sense lies. He writes:

> There are, indeed, things that cannot be put into words. They make themselves manifest. They are what is mystical.

The most common attempted solution to the evil problem rests on free will: the Free Will Defence. Free will has its own problems, discussed in the next chapter; but accepting, for now, that the concept of free will makes sense, how does it help? Defence of evil on the basis of free will does not, of course, deal easily with natural evils, unless, as some believe, natural evils arise because of evils emanating from human beings. The defence seeks primarily to solve the problem of moral evils, sufferings inflicted by humans.

Were God to ensure the world evil-free, the world would lack creatures with free will. Instead, there would be robots, human automata, programmed to perform the good. Robotic life necessarily possesses less value than lives of free agents – so it is assumed. God therefore created us as free agents, free then to do wrong as well as right – and, sadly, we often choose the wrong. That freedom provides individuals with opportunities for betterment, to grow morally – in this vale of Soul-making – and the possibility of eternal salvation. Pain, according to some Christians, is a privilege, uniting us with the redemptive suffering of Christ.

Any defence of evil on the basis of free will casts doubt on God's own goodness. Is God free to choose whether to perform good deeds? If he possesses such freedom, then, it seems, he must be capable of doing bad things. Some religious believers would reject that divine capacity. If he lacks such freedom, then he merits the robotic tag, robotic on a grand scale. Either way, there is once again mystery regarding the relationship between God and morality. Further mystery follows.

On the one hand, if God is a necessary being, whose characteristics are necessary, then the created world and its sufferings necessarily flow from him. Arguably, we ought not then to praise God for acting righteously, if he could do no other. Further, we may doubt whether human beings are ever free, if all their actions are necessitated, emanating from God; and if freedom is lacking, then, it seems, moral praise and blame would be unjustified. If what I choose is already determined by outside causes, how can I be held morally responsible?

On the other hand, if sense can be made of God having freely created this world of free agents, and if God is omniscient, then he would have known what the free agents would do. Free will is not incompatible with foreknowledge. In view of his foreknowledge, we may ask why God failed to create humans he knew would freely act well, instead creating ones who act so badly. It is no good reply that the beings would not then have been acting freely. If God can create free agents who end up behaving badly, he could have created free agents who end up behaving well.

Whichever way believers turn, puzzlements arise regarding God, as traditionally understood, and the evils of the world. For religious believers, that mystery is lived; it needs to be accepted. For humanists, the mystery points to morality's existence not being god-dependent.

'God is dead'

In 1882, Friedrich Nietzsche famously made the startling announcement above. With increased scientific understanding of worldly ways, there seemed no place for God. Despite that, God's shadow lingered in morality, as lawmaker – for example, with continuing references to Christ's 'do unto others'. People perhaps felt the need for God; maybe they took leaps of faith, as associated with Søren Kierkegaard. Leaps of faith – hops, skips or jumps – are, though, dangerous; into what may we be leaping? 'Put your trust in God, in Jesus Christ.' Is that rational? We must, according to Nietzsche, face up to our own choices, no longer relying on the myth of a Supreme Being as commander.

Nietzsche urges us not to believe 'those who speak of other-worldly hopes', but to be 'faithful to the earth'. That does not mean living according to nature, as per the Stoics. Nietzsche writes:

Think of a being such as nature, prodigal beyond measure, without
aims or intentions, indifferent beyond measure, without mercy
or justice, at once fruitful and barren and uncertain; think of
indifference itself as a power – how could you live according to
such indifference? To live – is that not precisely wanting to be
other than this nature?

With nature of no help, and with God no longer, 'Everything is
permitted'. That nihilistic aphorism is from Ivan, of Dostoevsky's
The Brothers Karamazov: without religion, morality holds no sway.
Nietzsche, though, was no nihilist; he urged instead a 'transvalu-
ation' of inherited Christian values.

Man is conceived, by Nietzsche, as a rope over an abyss, tied
between beast and a being beyond man, the Übermensch, a being
who affirms life, who values greatness. Nietzsche asked, indeed,
whether anyone can truly flourish surrounded by the numerous
miseries of others, even by one person suffering. The forthcoming
Übermensch will flourish; instead of drowning in pity, he finds
greatness. The nature of the Übermensch remains a mystery. Well,
Nietzsche did predict that he would not be understood for two
hundred years; we have fewer than a hundred to go.

Contrary to Nietzsche, the rejection of God as moral lawgiver
need not establish the vacuity of religion, requiring its demise.
Religious belief may help expose errors in viewing human
relations as means to ends, as commercial-like. The obligations
between parents and children, between lovers, are devalued if seen
in that economist way. The marriage 'contract', properly valued,
is no contract as if between punter and bookie. Religious rituals
can also enhance community cohesion and values such as self-
sacrifice, humility and providing sanctuary for the hounded. St
John Chrysostrom, fourth-century Archbishop of Constantinople,
drew attention to how the very wealthy had a moral duty to the
poor. Islam promotes Zakat, that is, regular alms-giving.

Of course, religion is far from necessary for appreciating the distinctiveness of human relationships and values; non-believers may grow their moral sensitivities through literature, art, music – through myths, while accepting them as myths; through psycho-analytical interpretations, whether treated as revealing realities or not. Religions, arguably more so than psychoanalytic theories, give rise to some seemingly surreal ideas: for example, atonement, where Christ's suffering – 'The cup which my Father hath given me, shall I not drink it?' – makes amends for our sins. According to certain Islamic beliefs, apostates should be killed. Sometimes there are religious endorsements of caste systems.

Those factors mentioned above – from dangerous irrationalities to serious oppression of wrong believers and non-believers to horrendous religiously inspired deaths for blasphemers – lead many humanists to shy completely away from all religion. Those human-ists ought not, though, to fall for the idea that the scientific under-standing of matters is therefore the only true understanding; there is, as just mentioned, an understanding acquired through the arts.

Neither the scientific view of the world nor religious scripture has the final word. The final word comes down to human inter-preters, to human evaluations. Such interpretation and evaluation may rightly see more in the world than that seen through the eyes of science and analysis; and religions give voice to that. Just as we view human behaviour and human faces as indicative of centres of consciousness with their own perspective on the world, so those religiously inclined experience nature – *Nature* – as the face of a benevolent God, despite the sufferings and horrors.

Here is Wittgenstein on the difficulties:

> An honest religious thinker is like a tightrope walker. He almost looks as though he were walking on nothing but air. His support is the slenderest imaginable. And yet it really is possible to walk on it.

It is obviously possible to live the religious life, some 'hocus-pocus', commented Maynard Keynes, as it is to live the non-religious, the humanist life – and in both cases to live the good life. Or is it? If a hold on truth, rather than mere sincere belief, is essential to good living, then one of the lives is certainly deficient, if one insists that God is a real presence and the other insists not.

$$\Upsilon$$

Even if God exists – or gods exist – and moral values are divinely grounded, we should still need to judge whether, and how, to accept them. If God does not exist, then whatever other moral injunctions we encounter, we need again to judge whether to defy or accept. That responsibility for our own judgements is existentialism's focus, to which we now turn.

Existentialists do not pass the moral buck to others, even to an Other Divine.

6
Existentialism: freedom and responsibility

We blame the hurricane when it uproots the ancient oak, kick the bicycle for its flat tyre and shout at the Siamese cat as it chases the pigeons, yet there is no serious conjecture that the hurricane, bicycle or feline is morally blameworthy. We know them as causally responsible, partly so, for the tragedies that unfold – they help bring them about – yet they engaged no reflection, weighed no factors; they moved without reason. How different it is, we assume, with human beings.

Human beings are usually held morally responsible for what they do; hence, they are usually – and ought to be – treated differently from other worldly items, animate or inanimate. We may open the door to welcome a guest, but not, unless metaphorically or humorously, a gust of wind. We praise the skills of the tightrope walker; we neither admire nor condemn the tightrope. Tightropes – hurricanes, bicycles and cats – are not recipients of moral evaluations. They know no shame; they know no absence of shame. There are grey areas, most obviously manifest in children.

We are entering the territory of reason and freedom of action. Moral demands apply only to those who can deliberate, choose and realize responsibility for resultant actions – to moral agents, to those who can act freely. For existentialists, freedom is central.

More accurately, central is their emphasis on the responsibility that we humans must accept in our doings and valuations. Existentialists do not confine their philosophizing to classrooms, tutorials or ivory towers. They live their philosophy.

Later in this chapter we confront the metaphysical question of whether we are ever free and hence ever merit moral praise or blame. First, though, we view prominent landmarks in the existentialists' territory, better to grasp existentialism's approach to morality.

Nothing prevents us...

Existentialism is a broad church: some existentialists are religious believers; many are not. Notable existentialists – more accurately, existentialism's forerunners – are Kierkegaard and Nietzsche, both of the nineteenth century. The existentialist label was first used by the twentieth-century Gabriel Marcel, and embraced famously by Jean-Paul Sartre and his long-standing companion Simone de Beauvoir, both influential intellectuals and political activists of mid-twentieth-century France.

Existentialists highlight individual responsibility. Humans are estranged from the world, either expressly or with the estrangement submerged. The estrangement arises through the incongruity between us as embodied biology and as conscious reflective beings, aware of our embodiment, needing to interpret the world and choose how to live. There exists a tension between seeing ourselves as part of the natural whole, the order of physical causes and effects, and as separate from that whole, transcending it, making free choices. That is, humans possess, in Sartre's terms, both facticity and transcendence. The two are intimate: we understand the factual world through our human purposes, practices and choices, features that appear to transcend the factual world of physics. Another tension arises between the individual and the community: we can rebel against the community herd of which we are part.

Existentialists are not intrinsically irrationalists. They reason about the matters above, set on understanding reality as it appears phenomenologically – as experienced in consciousness. They conclude that there is no reason for the universe; there is no reason, independent of our choices, which grounds our valuations. Camus – existentialist without label – points to how we long for reason behind the world, but the world is inscrutable, impenetrable and mysterious; there is no remedy. We are alienated not just from the physical causal world, but also from others and indeed from ourselves, from our physicality, emotions and experiences. Indeed, the poet Rilke wrote, 'We are not very much at home in this world that we have expounded.' Decades earlier, Novalis, an eighteenth-century German Romantic, spoke of philosophers seeking a homecoming, trying to feel at home in the world, in harmony and not alienated.

Consciousness reveals our freedom and our inescapable responsibility for handling the estrangement. Our choices and actions manifest our valuations, *our* valuations, *our* responsibility. Morality is not, however, determined by our feelings – a contrast with the next chapter's emotivists – for we are free to interpret our feelings, to respond to things differently. We may see our lover's behaviour, engrossed in conversation with another man, as disloyal; we experience jealousy. We may, though, see that same behaviour as compassionate; we experience admiration.

Understanding our place, or rather lack of place, in nature, existentialists encounter an ineluctable absurdity and feeling of abandonment; our responsibility cannot be shifted to others, however hard we try. Anxiety, *angst*, is the result – a dizziness of freedom. Nothing prevents us from jumping off a cliff. We could leap. Nothing prevents us from abandoning our family. We could walk out. Of course, we can seek to blind ourselves to the angst – to such possibilities – and we usually do.

To live authentically, eyes open, not in self-deception, we must recognize explicitly our freedom and responsibility. That realization can even be a joyful liberation. In the words of Kierkegaard, we individuals are 'constantly in the process of becoming', becoming aware of the existence of new possibilities for how we can be. As de Beauvoir portrays it, we are narratives on the world: we seek to construct a unity to our lives out of fragmentary episodes.

Condemned to be free

With that brief background, let us focus on Sartre's position: there is no God; there are no moral rules that bind us; there is no human nature that determines us. To think otherwise is a self-deception. As Sartre writes:

> … we have neither behind us, nor before us in a luminous realm of values, any means of justification or excuse. We are left alone, without excuse. That is what I mean when I say that man is condemned to be free. Condemned, because he did not create himself, yet is nevertheless at liberty, and from the moment that he is thrown into the world he is responsible for everything that he does.

For a human being, there is a future to be fashioned, 'a virgin future that awaits him'. No authority can be responsible for that future other than our own authority.

The existentialist emphasis on responsibility does not, in fact, require commitment to God's non-existence or, indeed, the non-existence of a realm of values. The emphasis on choice is as much present whether God exists, whether a realm of values exists. Suppose there is a God, suppose there is that realm: we still must choose whether to follow God's word, whether to commit to the values. We can be defiant. We can rebel. Abraham could have dismissed God's angel and the demand to sacrifice his son Isaac. Of course, there is a difference between saying that there are no values save those we create through our choices and saying that there are values, yet we choose whether to accept or dismiss them. In both cases, we remain responsible for our choices and actions.

Man has no function, no essential nature or purpose. To highlight this, Sartre distinguishes between being-in-itself (*l'être-en-soi*), where a function is determined, and being-for-itself (*l'être-pour-soi*), where there is consciousness, with nothing determined. An inkwell is known through what it is for: to hold ink. Its essence, its function to hold ink, precedes its existence. For man, things are reversed: existence precedes essence. I have no function or fixed nature; I am no *thing*. Although embodied, I am conscious, aware of my freedom – my freedom to value some things, disvalue others. To indicate that values are absent from the world, Sartre terms them 'ideal'.

Sartre seems to view choosing as grounded in an empty will, a will, as Iris Murdoch proposes, that is footloose, isolated from belief, reason and feeling – an empty, giddy will, totally unhinged from everything. Sartre writes:

> … my freedom is the unique foundation of values and *nothing*,
> absolutely nothing, justifies me in adopting this or that value,
> this or that scale of values. As the being by whom values exist,
> I am unjustifiable.

Caveats and explanations are needed to prevent this from being utterly mysterious; yet caveats and explanations detract from the alluring obscurity of Sartre's literary expression, for example, his 'nothingness lies coiled in the heart of being, like a worm'.

With detraction to the fore, we note the obvious truth that human beings have biological parts that operate in unchosen ways. No human being can live the way of a fish – or soar unaided to the Moon – yet, of course, a person lacks the fixity of an inkwell.

We can sense, at least on the surface, how a person is free, within limits, to choose how to live. Sartre's freedom is not meant to be arbitrary, capricious or random. Existentialist choices are not really derived *ex nihilo*, from nothing. We are orientated within a situation, yet our attitudes are not thereby determined.

In summary: biology constrains choices; biology does not make choices. As Sartre later puts it, 'You can always make something out of what you've been made into.' He says, for example, 'I cannot be crippled without choosing myself as crippled.' I choose the way in which I treat my disability – whether humiliating, something to flaunt or something to use. We can orientate.

Obscurity remains. Whether existentialist or not – how are our orientations, choices, interpretations grounded, yet also made freely? If grounded in nothing, they would appear to be random; if grounded in something outside, we should not have determined them ourselves. We are entering the free will puzzle; but before that explicit engagement, let us grasp more of Sartre's morality.

The waiter – in bad faith?

How man lives shows what it is that he values. How man lives is his responsibility. To believe otherwise is to enter a self-deception, *mauvais fois*, bad faith. Here is the much-discussed waiter tale, a tale Sartre probably wrote while in *Les Deux Magots* in Saint-Germain, Paris:

> His movement is quick and forward, a little too precise, a little too rapid. He comes toward the customers with a step a little too quick. He bends forward a little too eagerly; his voice, his eyes express an interest a little too solicitous for the order of the client. Finally there he returns, trying to imitate in his walk the inflexible stiffness of some kind of automaton while carrying his tray with the recklessness of a tightrope-walker by putting it in

a perpetually unstable, perpetually broken equilibrium which he perpetually re-establishes by a light movement of the arm and hand.

The man is trying to secure himself as a being-in-itself, as a café-waiter-object, determined by its function. It is as if there is no free choice involved in his rising at dawn, no free choice in his conferring value on the rights and duties of a waiter. In Sartre's paradoxical terminology, he is not a waiter in the mode of a being-in-itself, but is a waiter in the mode of what he is not. 'We are what we are not and are not what we are.'

The example reminds us that our choices are indeed determined in part by our biology. If no other work is available, yes, the man has a choice, between working as a waiter or starving – that is, between living or not living at all. That choice differs somewhat from the choice between committing to a political party or gardening or philosophizing.

As observers of the waiter, we, the public, may see his behaviour as a game, yet we may connive. In bad faith, we reify ourselves as customers and him as waiter. We have expectations regarding such social roles:

there is the dance of the grocer, of the tailor, of the auctioneer, by which they endeavour to persuade their clientele that they are nothing but a grocer, an auctioneer, a tailor. A grocer who dreams is offensive to the buyer, because such a grocer is not wholly a grocer.

The man – as waiter, grocer or tailor – may indeed be playing the part of a mechanism, really denying his freedom; he is hence in bad faith. We may similarly be in bad faith; we fix ourselves as diners.

Rather than being in bad faith, the man, the so-called waiter, could, though, be consciously seeing his actions as a game, as play, as could we when playing at being customers. Whether the

THE FOLLY OF RELATIVISM

Existentialists reap accusations that they treat values as resting on choice or taste. If you feel subjectively that something is right, then it is right. That is a limiting case of *moral relativism*: morality is relative to the subject. Relativism is often cultural. Slavery was right for ancient Athens, it is said, but is not for us today in the West.

'It's all relative, isn't it?' No. Some argue that all truths are relative – true *for him* or *for his culture*, but not thereby true *for us*. That is nonsense. This book will not turn into an elephant – that is an objective truth. If an express train runs you over, you will be injured – no relative matter at all.

Relativism is often restricted to morality: if someone tortures you for fun, that is only relatively wrong; such torture could be right *for that culture*. Nothing more can be said by us against it. Yet if the students' mathematics answers are wrong, is it just a relative matter that I ought to give lower grades than otherwise? Is it just a relative matter that it is wrong to torment the sick?

Stoning for adultery: In certain Islamic states, women guilty of adultery are sentenced to death by stoning. Cultural relativists may argue that such treatment is wrong in the West, but right for Islamic states. *Hence*, we have no right to intervene or protest. That conclusion fails to follow. If moral matters are just relative, then perhaps, relative to our society, we ought to intervene.

Toleration or respect? Moral relativists may be intending to defend toleration, but that we should be tolerant is a moral claim, not itself relative. Valuing liberty, we may insist that, morally, people ought to be allowed to live as they want so long as not harming others. Of course, there are questions: does denigrating people pass muster as harm?

We ought not to tolerate genocide, but should we tolerate those who merely declare in speech their support for it? Perhaps we should tolerate intolerable views being expressed – holocaust denial, for example – but that does not mean we should respect those views or even have much respect for the purveyors thereof. Not all views deserve respect.

example is one of bad faith therefore depends on what the waiter is up to. In fact, play for Sartre is contrasted with seriousness: man is serious when he takes himself for an object, hiding his freedom. If I insist seriously that I am not a coward, I may be implying that I am something else, something fixed – more bad faith.

Here is a question. What is so bad about bad faith, in individuals deceiving themselves, closing eyes to their human freedom, be it through identifying with a role, succumbing to how others perceive them or excusing their actions as caused by external events? Surprisingly, Sartre condemns such deception; yet on his approach, valuing good faith should have no greater objectivity than valuing bad faith – for we are free to choose our values.

Sartre's defence is, he says, 'grounded in logic'. The player in bad faith is hiding from reality; he acts in error. Strict consistency demands that we recognize our freedom; and with such recognition we act in good faith. We could respond that Sartre should see nothing objectively wrong in embracing error and inconsistency. Why not self-deceive, if it makes life easier? Errors of self-deception may be preferable to any veridical angsts of freedom.

Clearly then, Sartre's existentialism is not intended as a simple nihilism of 'anything goes'. Sartre values authenticity. At one stage, he steps even further into recognizable moral terrain, with a Kantian universalizing spin:

> Once a man has seen that values depend upon himself, in that state
> of forsakenness he can will only one thing, and that is freedom
> as the foundation of all values.

In choosing, I create what I value; I therefore value for all of mankind, at least in as far as choosing shows that I value freedom. Sartre's universalizing, as he later saw, sits uneasily with the rest of his existentialism. Recognizing my freedom means I recognize the freedom of others; but why should I value reciprocal freedom, honouring that freedom of others?

An approach by de Beauvoir casts some light. A person's existence is degraded into an in-itself – a mere object – when bad faith succeeds. In bad faith, I let my freedom lapse into facticity; my transcendence of the physical world collapses into immanence, into the physical world. I deceive myself by objectifying myself, an object with a fixed nature – a waiter, an automaton. That is a moral fault when we consent to it in ourselves. Therefore it is a moral fault when we inflict it on others; it amounts to oppression.

We could resist that conclusion, even while accepting that bad faith degrades ourselves. We could be authentic in our commitment to oppressing others, turning them into objects. That may yet commit a deeper metaphysical error. For me to have a sense of *my* self, I need the presence of others. Sartre describes this vividly via 'the Look': I become aware of myself through the gaze of others. That is vague, but gestures at the following.

What dignity do I achieve, what status do I possess, if the sole 'admiration' I receive is from slaves whom I oppress, whom I treat as mere objects? I cannot be valued by a tractor, admired by a pebble or feel shame before a tree; and I cannot be respected by others, if I order them to respect me and, from fear, they move *as if* respectful. A human being, a being-for-itself, could not exist completely divorced from free agents or, at least, their possibility. At best, though, that shows only my need to acknowledge and respect the existence of *some* other free agents; it does not show why I ought not to oppress anyone at all.

The student

Freedom is the essence of consciousness; anguish is the consciousness of freedom. Hence, we exist in anguish. We often mask that anguish, as seen, through self-deception, hiding responsibility for our choices.

In 1940s Paris, under German occupation, a student sought Sartre's advice. The student's lonely mother was ailing; she lived only for him. Her elder son, his brother, had been killed by the occupying force. The student felt the full weight of needing to stay with his mother. He was, though, torn. He wanted to avenge his brother's death. At a public level, he wanted to combat the occupation. He should flee to England, join the Free French Forces and then return to fight. Yes, helping his mother would have the immediacy of making her life better. Yes, the project of fighting might end in failure, 'vanishing like water into sand', yet he felt the demand to avenge. The student had to choose.

The student had to choose between two courses. He sought advice; yet, on existentialist reasoning, how would any advice help? First, to which advisers should he listen? Secondly, advisers may give conflicting advice – and how do they reach their advice? Thirdly, whatever advice is given, assuming consistent, he has still to decide whether to follow it. He may decide to do his duty; but what determines his duty? He may decide to follow his gut feelings, but how does he weigh feelings?

Sartre responded, arguably unhelpfully. He offered no views on the particular considerations; any views, he seemed to think, could have no bearing on the student's decision. He apparently simply said:

You are free, therefore choose – that is to say, invent.

Given that response, the tale is usually taken to present the world as valueless until we choose. Yet does it show that? Value judgements exist in the dilemma from the beginning. The student recognizes the evils of the occupation, the significance of his mother's need and his perceived duty regarding his brother's death. His dilemma arises because those recognized values compete; they are all values of significance to him. The dilemma is not as if a trivial choice between wearing a red dress and a blue. It is not to be settled by spins of a coin. He wants to make the right choice.

That there is a choice is right, but that it is a choice to be made without scope for reasoning, advice, talking through, is wrong. Discussion could have helped the student see his motives and values more clearly. That would not have made the choice for him, but he might have found himself more in tune with one way of looking, with putting his personal duty above duties of the political – or vice versa.

'You'd face a coward in the mirror each day you stayed at home,' he may have thought, then adding, 'Yes, but that could be the courageous path.' If he remained with his mother, maybe he would be judged too scared to fight; so, he needed courage to handle public humiliation. Or perhaps he needed to stand up to his mother's tears, as he said goodbye, convinced that he must avenge his brother's death.

In making his choice he is, in a sense, making himself. (The idea is explored in Chapter Ten.) When he sought to do what is right, he sought to do what is right for him. That does not imply that any choice made would be right so long as he felt it right. To have skulked around, helping neither his mother nor the Resistance – but to have played cards night after night – would not have been right. For him, though, it may have been right to stay with his mother; for someone else, to join the Resistance. Contrary to Sartre's earlier injunction, to choose for him is not thereby to choose for all. It is, though, to choose without excuse. It is, as Sartre said, to create – to invent – himself.

Nothing more than complex thermostats?

The existence of free choice has been assumed. Moral praise and blame surely are deserved only if we possess the freedom to choose to attempt the action or not. We need therefore to take seriously the argument that all actions are causally determined by past events grounded in our nature and nurture over which we lacked ultimate control; hence no choice is free choice, no action free action. Given the circumstances, we could not have chosen otherwise than we did, so we ought not to be held morally responsible; we merit neither moral praise nor blame.

We accept people as responsible for their actions when they are the originating cause of what they do. We excuse people, when they are compelled to act by external factors: by gunmen, hypnotists or drugs. Some internal factors also excuse people: they may have a compulsive neurosis, so are blameless. In listing excusing factors, we are casually assuming that there exists a 'true' chooser, a true actor morally responsible when excusing factors are absent. The question becomes: should the fact (if it is one) that our actions are causally determined, being events in causal chains that stretch back before our existence, be added to the excusing list?

Our development is determined by our genetic make-up (we certainly did not choose that) and by our environment, culture, education and training; we did not initially control those. 'But some children choose to work hard; others do not.' Hard-working inclinations, though, are also presumably caused by genetic make-up, upbringing and environmental impingings. Just as we may be at the mercy of the gunman, the hypnosis or drugs, are we not, even more so, at the mercy of the causally deterministic world?

There seems no escape from concluding that moral praise and blame is unjustified; there is, though, one attempted escape: indeterminism. Perhaps the world is not completely deterministic. That 'solution' to the free will problem – that, at the micro level of quantum mechanics, indeterminism, randomness reigns – is no solution at all. Free choices are not meant to be random events that happen to us. Further, it is no help thinking of actions being partly determined, for what of the undetermined part? That part, being undetermined, leaves us adrift in random seas.

Consider a thermostat. It lacks free will. Even if we add a voice box, even if the programme contains random elements, we should not hold the thermostat responsible for what it does.

The arising moral muddles are illustrated by the loutish teenagers caught by Officer Krupke; they are facing the judge. Seeking to evade responsibility for their misdeeds, the teenagers insist:

> It's our upbringing that gets us out of hand;
> we can't help it, you need to understand.

They could have added that their genes, brain structures and culture also contributed to their bad behaviour, all factors beyond their control; so, they could not possibly be morally responsible or held accountable. The judge could respond that he is terribly sorry, but given his judgemental upbringing and neurology, he cannot help but sentence them to ten years imprisonment – and hard labour.

The institution of desert, of what is deserved, of praise and blame, of our judicial systems – if requiring free will as so far understood – rests on a mistake. Our moral censures may be as inappropriate as medieval animal trials, where pigs, wolves and rats would be found guilty of misdeeds and sentenced accordingly. Praise and blame, on this view, amount at best to manipulative inputs to secure certain consequences. We select punishments, moral exhortations, prizes, if likely to generate desirable future behaviour. Hospitals and straitjackets come into play when moral evaluations and pressures are ineffective. Of course, if determinism does hold, then our desires regarding future behaviour are outside our control – as are our arguments about determinism. How logical reasoning, good reasoning, relates to neurological causes and effects in which it is grounded remains a deep metaphysical puzzle.

Let us reflect. *Must* we live with the sceptical conclusion that no one truly merits moral assessment? Here are two thoughts for moving forward. The first concerns lack of sense; the second proposes a different approach.

Free will, understood as 'could have done otherwise in exactly the same circumstances', or as requiring agents to be in ultimate control, is surely incoherent, senseless. We should no more fret about its lack of sense than fret about the lack of round squares or how to 'blibble-blobble' – that expression being senseless. Free will, as understood so far, can exist neither in deterministic nor inde-terministic worlds. Even its logical possibility has been excluded.

If *I*, to act freely, must be understood as not characterized by any features ultimately derived from outside my control, then I am featureless, an existentialist nothing. The self, the 'I', vanishes. If I am more than nothing – with dispositions of kindness, irrit-ability or preferences for red wine – then the sceptical challenge arises: the 'more' was brought about by factors outside my control. Ultimately I cannot be author of my existence; hence, I cannot be held morally responsible for anything.

For a different approach, let us turn to the everyday, where we do treat people as acting freely; that is, when they act as they want, from their convictions, for good reasons and so forth. If that is our starting point, we have the makings of a 'compatibil-ist' position – compatibilist because doing what we want, having reasons, is compatible with causal determinism. You fall into her arms because you want to – as opposed to because you tripped over the cat. In the first case, you acted freely; in the second, not. If you open the safe because you are after the cash, you act freely; if because a loaded gun is pressed against your head, you act under compulsion. In the latter case, your action is mixed: reason tells you what to do to survive, but you have no desire to aid the gunman.

The above line is far too coarse as it stands. People want to smoke; in smoking they do what they want, but they may deeply prefer to be non-smokers – so they are not really smoking freely. Their first-order desire to smoke is fulfilled, but their second-order desire, to be non-smokers, is thwarted. Free action may now be grasped as acting in accordance with second-order, or deeper-order, desires, desires that involve rationality and reflection about how we want our lives to go. We act freely when we identify what we do as in accord with how we want to make ourselves. Inevitably, there are grey areas, as we are about to see.

We know that we ought not to drink and drive, but such a duty, such rationality, is swamped by immediate desires; we succumb to more drinks. That is *akrasia*, weakness of will. Perhaps we should be blamed for such weakness – we could surely have resisted the swamping – yet akrasia can also be viewed as the very manifestation of lack of free will. Akrasia – often translated from the classics, unhappily so, as 'incontinence' – is described by Ovid thus:

> Some strange power draws me on against my will. Desire persuades me one way, reason another. I see the better course and approve it; I follow the worse.

How can that weakness arise? Socrates understood it as a failure to see matters clearly. Our eyesight for distant disasters – road accidents, throat cancer – is defective. Akrasia therefore should not be viewed as voluntary; we are acting in ignorance of the horrendous possibilities of our actions. If that is taken seriously, we reach an asymmetry, one already encountered in Kant's thinking: we act freely when doing what is right, but are always acting unfreely when doing what is wrong. In Aristotle's terms, akrasia is a failure in the practical wisdom necessary for being virtuous. Should we be held accountable for such failure, given that we are, so to speak, sleepwalking, unable to see clearly?

That we are aware of conflicts between our desires, that we can judge between them, sometimes resisting the easy route – that we have reasons for our choices – are marks of free action, marks distinctive of most human beings, of persons. Non-human animals lack such reflective decisions. They move according to their dominant desires. Some humans, 'wantons' – maybe all of us, on occasion – are just driven by the net outcome of conflicting desires, as flotsam moves according to the strongest currents. Often, though, we stand fast against the currents, being true to our deepest bedrock desires and values.

MORALITY: WITHOUT LUCK?

Moral luck is contradictory; surely we cannot be rightly blamed or praised for events outside our control – or can we?

What you bring about: Janet and John drive with the same degree of casual attentiveness. A child runs in front of John's car and is killed. Luckily, no child runs in front of Janet. What resulted from John's driving – a child killed – was outside John's control, yet people heap blame on John: he should have been more careful. Janet receives no blame. Is that differential treatment morally justified?

Decisions – and circumstances: Janet and John possess the same character traits. They both succumb to authority, wanting an easy life. Janet lives in a peaceful country, no horrendous demands on her. John lives in a dictatorial state; he must obey orders. We blame John for taking part in, say, genocide, or helping in the gas chambers – yet Janet would have done the same. If John merits blame, then surely so does Janet. Circumstances were outside John's control. Had he not been in Syria or Rwanda or Nazi Germany, he would have reaped no blame.

Nature and nurture: We push on further. The sort of individual you are – whether you are timid or strong, authoritarian or liberal – are surely matters of genetic or educational luck. How can it be right to blame, say, Ms Ruthless, unluckily possessed of a ruthless nasty character? She did not choose her nature and nurture. Mr Peaceful inherited a kindly character; but does he merit praise for that good fortune?

Puzzles: John regrets being a driver who killed – 'agent regret' – even though not his fault. His tragedy is that he killed. It was his bad luck, yet he accepts moral responsibility; after all, he killed a child.

Turning to bad luck as excusing our character, a response is: identity precedes luck and unluck. Before questions of luck arise, we must exist with a certain nature, making us who we are. We do not merit praise or blame for coming into existence. Mind you, that we exist is surely astonishing luck, be it for good or ill.

My attitude is towards a soul

The compatibilist approach to free will has obvious problems. The truly wicked cannot help being the sort of people they are, with their deepest desires being for wickedness. We cannot help which desires we happen to have. Moral accolades received rest upon a range of bad to good fortunes – on moral luck (please see 'Morality: without luck?', p. 117). The basic puzzle reappears: our moral judgements of people seem bereft of good grounds.

David Hume asked whether it was possible to live the life of the sceptic, of one who doubted everything. He thought not. If truly sceptical, you would have no reason to eat or drink – why think they are sensible activities? You would have no need to avoid cliff tops: who can tell whether falling will again be dangerous? The true sceptics would have short lives, unless with non-sceptical friends who tend them, steering them away from cliff tops.

Here we ask: is it possible to live a life, treating all actions as causally determined, with no one held morally responsible? Think of everyday human attitudes. We readily recognize distinctions between living creatures and objects – and between human beings and other creatures. The proposal is that we cannot live a human life without treating each other as persons, typically morally responsible. Further, we do not usually treat others as doubtfully known points of consciousness hidden behind biological masks, the human form. As Wittgenstein expresses that point:

> My attitude towards him is an attitude towards a soul. I am not of the opinion that he has a soul.

We can see that someone is in pain or is deliberately standing in our way – that there is a person present, no mere object. In the words of Simone Weil:

If we step aside for a passer-by on the road, it is not the same thing as stepping aside to avoid a billboard; alone in our rooms, we get up, walk about, sit down again quite differently from the way we do when we have a visitor.

We respect other human beings in moving aside; they possess powers to refuse what we demand, not as a key that refuses to turn in a lock. We often need consent from others; we seek no consent from locks. That need registers awareness of others as deserving respect and fair treatment. Indeed, my treating others as slaves, as puppets, as mere physical impediments, may, as seen earlier (p. 110), undermine respect for myself.

We may humiliate a person, but not a boulder or tree. We blush with embarrassment, admire someone's skill; no cat blushes or admires. We love and forgive, feel indignant or angry, show gratitude or admiration. Those relationships matter. Do others have good will towards us – or are they malevolent? The attitudes are 'reactive attitudes'. We could not live a human life without such reactive attitudes, without treating people as moral agents.

Reactive attitudes can be suspended. People sometimes act so bizarrely, dangerously even, that they are incapable of normal personal relationships; we may then adopt objective attitudes, neither praising nor blaming, but seeking medical treatment for those people. That is the radical case of moral suspension. Minor cases occur: their behaviour was not the result of bad will, but accidental; they escape blame. When we adopt objective attitudes to people, we still do not view them as nothing but physical objects. We still care about them and for them; we attempt to re-engage them in reactive relationships.

The proposal that we cannot conduct lives while believing in determinism and its incompatibility with moral relationships, may yet be challenged. If we were, one day, to discover physical determinants of all human behaviour, we should surely lose sight of free will and moral responsibility. Yet would – or could – our behaviour change in any significant way?

Even if I know my actions are causally determined, I still have to choose what to do next and how to react to others. Possibly, I could become so psychologically detached that I treat other people as nothing but causal sources, hindering me or providing me with pleasures – no different from the wind blowing me off course or the sun allowing me to bask – but I should still have to treat *myself* as a choice-making agent. Perhaps that is why we see an asymmetry between the past – totally fixed – and the future, open to deliberation; inevitably I have to make choices about the future. Further – and doubting Sartre's 'nothingness' – to make sense of my actions, plans and projects, I must treat myself as something enduring, with a past, with a future, not as a nothing – otherwise I should have no reason for doing anything about myself at all.

♈

Whatever reality exists behind our concepts of a persisting self, of choice and free action, the demands of morality may yet be illusory. It may simply be prudent sometimes to acquiesce in so-called morality, other times to rebuff. No values exist with a justified hold over us. Or is that so?

We need to give the moral sceptics a run for their money. This takes us into considerations of meta-ethics, of what is meant by our moral terms, of how moral properties do (or do not) exist. Meta-ethics and moral scepticism can entwine, as Schopenhauer observed:

> The theoretical examination of the foundation of morals is open to the quite peculiar disadvantage that it is easily regarded as an undermining thereof, which might entail the collapse of the structure itself.

7

Morality: just an illusion?

Look around the world. You see lakes, forests and oceans, mountains and molehills, deserts, ice-cream desserts and rats. You see stars shimmering, snowflakes falling, and maybe a red sky in the morning. There are colours, shapes, sounds and aromas: heavy rains, lightning flashes, yet elsewhere parched grasses. Do you spy – do you hear, touch, taste or scent – objects or properties such as goodness and rightness, distinct from the objects with their colours, shapes and aromas?

Let us focus on people. We slip on the ice, become burned by the sun or excited by the music. We meet people with aims and ambitions, some wealthy, numerous in poverty, many in between. We notice children playing without a care, others suffering ravages of war, starvation. Do we sense any moral properties, such as goodness and badness, properties that fix what we morally *must*, or *must not*, do?

Suppose we conduct scientific investigations, be they of human brains, behaviour or ways of natural selection. Would we encounter atoms of rightness, atoms of wrongness, or some properties of good, others of bad? Is morality grounded in the world external to us – or within our brains or even deeper within – such that scientific investigations could reveal what we morally ought or ought not to do?

One answer is a seemingly simple 'no' – well, it is 'no' until nuances are highlighted. The answer manifests the is/ought dichotomy, already encountered, associated with David Hume:

> In every system of morality, which I have hitherto met with, I
> have always remarked, that the author proceeds for some time
> in the ordinary way of reasoning, and establishes the being of a
> God, or makes observations concerning human affairs; when of
> a sudden I am surprized to find, that instead of the usual copula-
> tions of propositions, *is*, and *is not*, I meet with no proposition
> that is not connected with an *ought*, or an *ought not*.

Hume's point here is that neither reasoning nor evidence of the
senses, nor scientific investigation, can move us legitimately from
descriptions of what *is* so to prescriptions or evaluations about
what *ought* to be so. Even though Lavinia *is* suffering, that alone
does not show that morally we *ought* to help. In the end, Hume
bases morality on our sentiments; we feel for her – and that is
why we help.

Does a gulf exist between 'is' and 'ought'? If so, is there a
bridge enabling us to cross? (Let us remember: when an action
is morally right, there resides an 'ought' lurking within). Kant
saw reason as providing the bridge; Mill attempted a proof or at
least some apposite considerations (please see the insert, p. 123).
Many, though, stand firm on the Humean ground that 'ultimate
ends of human actions can never be accounted for by reason, but
recommend themselves entirely to the sentiments and affections
of mankind'. Hume adds:

> Reason is, and ought only to be the slave of the passions, and
> can never pretend to any other office than to serve and obey
> them… It is not contrary to reason to prefer the destruction of
> the whole world to the scratching of my finger.

Morality as grounded in biology has been met within virtue
ethics, though that approach sometimes proposes values, such
as justice, that are not obviously 'nothing more' than certain
natural feelings. A strong naturalism tells us that moral properties

A PROOF OF WHAT IS GOOD AND RIGHT...?

John Stuart Mill's test for an action's rightness is whether it promotes the good. Here is his 'proof' of what is good:

> The only proof capable of being given that an object is visible, is that people actually see it. The only proof that a sound is audible, is that people hear it... In like manner, the sole evidence it is possible to produce that anything is desirable, is that people do desire it. No reason can be given why the general happiness is desirable, except that each person, so far as he believes it attainable, desires his own happiness... Thus, happiness is a good: each person's happiness is a good to that person, and the general happiness, therefore, a good to the aggregate of all persons.

Mill's 'proof' has received objections such as those that follow; but some of them seem wrongly to take him as offering a formal deduction rather than points in favour of a utilitarian approach.

Desirability: Just because something is desired, it does not follow it is desirable, in the sense of 'worthy of desire'. People desire undesirable things. Mill may point out that he is merely arguing that what people desire simply affords *some* evidence, not conclusive evidence, for the desired items being worthy of desire.

A mistaken generalization: Suppose Mill is right: we each desire our happiness and it is worthy of desire; still, *ought* we to aim at the happiness of others? That aim may conflict with our own happiness. Further, are my desires simply for happiness? I may desire the life of a conductor and it would be part of my happiness; but it fails to follow that I desire conducting *because* it is part of happiness. Consider an analogy: I want that painting and it belongs to Leya, but I do not thereby want the painting *because* it belongs to Leya.

Impossibility: Even if everything each person desires contributes to happiness, and happiness is worthy of desire, the general happiness may not be desirable; it may be impossible. There is nothing wrong in each player desiring to be captain, yet it is not desirable – it is usually impossible – for all players to be captain.

are literally identical with some natural properties; no bridge is required between the natural and the moral. Let us investigate.

To explain is neither to justify nor to explain away

The moral, some suggest, is determined by our natural instincts for human survival. That leads to a popular albeit confused reductionism of the moral to the natural.

Explanations are on offer for the evolution of species and their physical characteristics. Evolutionary psychology explains how certain human emotions developed. Crude models of organisms battling for survival fail to account for altruistic, moral behaviour; but plausible genetic accounts now exist. Unfortunately, the accounts sometimes lapse into unhappy metaphor – for instance, 'the selfish gene' of Richard Dawkins, who wrote, 'Let us try to teach generosity and altruism, because we are born selfish.' Of course, genes are not selfish. Even if they were, it would not follow that people are selfish or born selfish. Items need not possess features of their constituents; apples' constituents are swirling electrons, but apples themselves rarely swirl.

One danger from science is 'nothing buttery'. Moral behaviour is 'nothing but' certain replicating genes. Discovering causes, though, does not show that the item caused is 'nothing but' the causes. Whisky drinking caused her to miss the train, but the missing of the train differs from the drinking; the crown of a tree, points out the artist Paul Klee, is not a mirror of its roots. Better it is sometimes to know only the resultant fine work rather than its origins – as Thomas Mann averred regarding his novelette *Death in Venice*. There are natural selection and neurological explanations of our ability to see mountains and oceans, but those explanations neither account for which items exist to be seen, nor prove that these items are 'nothing but' neurological constructions. We should resist exotic claims such as 'morality resides in our neurology'. Morality no more exists in our neurology than do mountains.

Another tempting belief is that if moral behaviour can be explained – be it by evolution, genes or environment – then the behaviour cannot be truly moral. That needs challenging.

First, the explanation is proposed for the existence of moral behaviour; so it is curious that the conclusion undermines its existence. *To explain is not thereby to explain away.*

Secondly, some people conclude that evolutionary theory shows we are 'really' motivated to spread our genes; but few people think 'I must spread my genes tonight' – and, but for saving the theory, there is no reason to conclude such motivations exist unconsciously. *Saving a theory differs from discovering the truth.*

Thirdly, even if there are plausible evolutionary explanations for certain types of behaviour – why, for example, we have greater concern for relatives than strangers – we may reasonably respond, 'So? What does that show about how we *ought* to behave?' No doubt there are evolutionary explanations for why some men rape – maybe, one day, why some people believe in God, why some accept evolutionary theory – but those explanations would form neither justification for the behaviour and beliefs explained nor disproof of the beliefs. As Darwin pointed out, natural selection is not about moral betterment, but merely betterment as survival. *To explain is not to justify.*

Evolutionary explanations have been introduced to shore up global capitalism. Competitive capitalistic interactions, it has been argued, derive from features that enabled our predecessors to survive predators. Maybe that is true, but that does not justify capitalism as morally worthwhile. *What is evolutionarily adaptive is not thereby morally desirable.*

Here is a related muddle. Dawkins speaks of good Darwinian reasons for individuals sometimes to be moral; yet he also encourages rebellion against genetically grounded tendencies of ruthlessness and selfishness. No scientific explanation is being thereby given of why morally we should rebel in some cases, yet not in others. Scientific investigations cannot tell us that the survival of a species is valuable or even that we should disvalue cancerous cells. That we value finding the truth through scientific investigations is not itself justified by experimentation and scientific theory. *We bring valuations to science.*

With such reflections, we are gently entering meta-ethics; it is a 'meta' or higher-level study of morality. Here is an analogy. You are a mathematician, able to prove theorems in arithmetic and geometry. At a different level, you would investigate the nature of numbers and geometrical figures, what sort of existence they have – their ontological status. Similar to that 'different level', meta-ethics asks what is meant by moral expressions, whether moral properties exist, and, if so, how we know of them.

Everything is what it is – and not another thing

A highly influential twentieth-century challenge to naturalism appeared in G. E. Moore's *Principia Ethica*, a work that became the secular bible of the Bloomsbury Group, influencing Virginia Woolf, John Maynard Keynes and many more.

Moore introduced the Naturalistic Fallacy. Quite what constituted the fallacy, he later acknowledged, was obscure, moving between questions of meanings and the qualities of things. Without doubt, though, Moore was distinguishing between, on the one hand, the ethical dimension and on the other, the natural world and, indeed, the metaphysical world.

Moore focused on intrinsic goodness: what is good in itself. It is a fallacy to *identify* goodness with any natural properties, such as the greatest pleasure or that conducive to human survival. It is a fallacy to identify goodness with the metaphysical, such as states approved by God; the fallacy is as much metaphysical as naturalistic. It can be viewed as a definitional fallacy. Goodness is a property distinct from all others. Moore approved Joseph Butler's dictum: 'Everything is what it is and not another thing'. (We met Butler earlier, with his attack on Hobbes, p. 7.) Goodness, according to Moore, is a simple unanalysable property. Its lack of analysis is akin to yellowness's lack of analysis. The analogy, though, is not ideal: perhaps yellowness is analysable as certain wavelengths.

Although goodness is unanalysable and is neither natural nor metaphysical, it is a property. Moore's following 'open question' argument is meant to show this. Take any proposed definition, X, of goodness. Is it not always a significant question to ask, 'But is X good?' Suppose someone claims: goodness is identical with whatever promotes survival. It is significant to ask, 'Is promotion of survival always good?' We could move the questioning to 'right'. The right action must accord with the Categorical Imperative, says Kant. Yet surely it is significant to ask, 'Is such an action therefore right?'

The argument, so far, is far from impressive. After all, definitions can be informative – even the simple definition that a vixen is a female fox. Maybe Moore is driving at two important points. The first is that standard competent language users who correctly use the term 'good' will not typically accept filled-in instances of '… is what goodness is' – such as, 'Promotion of survival is what goodness is' – as true by virtue of the words' meanings. There will be an open question about them, argument about them.

The second point is that no method exists that could justifiably lead us to agree, 'Ah, that is what goodness is really.' The terms 'water' and 'H_2O' arguably have different meanings, but we discovered, through recognized procedures, that water just is H_2O, maybe even that water *must* be H_2O; indeed, that discovery influences current definitions of 'water'. What empirical evidence, what procedures, what reasoning, though, could settle what constitutes goodness? Similar rhetorical questions arise regarding any value, moral or aesthetic. As Plato notes, if we differ about the larger and smaller, measurements can settle matters; but differences over the just and unjust, the beautiful and ugly, the good and bad, can make people angry and hostile. No agreed measure exists.

Although Moore insisted that goodness is indefinable, he also said that goodness is 'what ought to exist for its own sake'. Presumably Moore's basic point is that goodness and related moral terms cannot be defined solely in non-moral terms, though they may be inter-defined. What is good, for example, determines which actions are right. Some things, of course, may be deemed 'good' because they are instruments for – means to – states intrinsically good. Suffering in the dentist's chair is good, but only as the necessary means to the intrinsic good of toothache absence.

Moore was driving at a nice, a subtle, point in his claim that goodness differs from all other non-moral properties, but he was no mystic; an item is good only because it possesses certain natural properties. In today's terminology, goodness 'supervenes' on the natural; supervenience provides the bridge between the moral and the natural. If there is a moral difference between two states, then there must be a difference in their natural properties. Moore even tells us what the relevant natural properties are; they are summed as personal affections and aesthetic enjoyments. If the same sort of natural personal affection exists in two cases, then it is not possible that only one of them has the further property, the supervening property, of goodness.

Moore's list of natural properties upon which goodness supervenes is revealed by clarity of intuition rather than reasoning about what contributes to human flourishing. They may appear a mishmash, an unsystematic medley with no underlying unity, but they are no worse for that. By way of criticism, though, we may perform a response akin to Moore's open question: we may ask, 'Are personal affections and aesthetic enjoyments states upon which intrinsic goodness supervenes?' Just as Moore doubted whether any investigation could lead us to agree that goodness 'just is' this or that, so we may doubt whether any investigation could lead us justly to agree that goodness must supervene on this or that.

Sighs may arise. After all the fuss concerning goodness not being a natural property, it transpires that it must supervene on certain natural properties. That seems an arcane point, one with its own difficulties. If goodness is a supervening but non-natural property, how are we acquainted with it? Must we postulate a special moral sense, a moral intuition, as we possess the sense of touch for hardness? Typical perception – seeing, hearing *et al.* – would appear to play no essential part for apprehending goodness given that it differs from all natural properties. Goodness does not seem to possess causal powers that enable us to perceive it. Perhaps reasoning, moral sensitivity or revelation could lead some to grasp that affection has the non-natural property of goodness, and that deliberate cruelty lacks that property, as do, presumably, bicycles and boulders. It is, though, all somewhat mysterious.

'It never occurred to me'

Moore, in understanding goodness to be a real property, is an ethical realist. Many view that commitment to non-natural moral properties as weird, certainly obscure. One escape from the darkness is to deny that goodness is a property at all. Maybe moral judgements are akin to expressions of emotion, attitude or feeling. When that suggestion was put to Moore, Moore, with disarming candour, said that the idea had never occurred to him. What he surely thought was that the idea was too ridiculous to have occurred to him. Perhaps, though, it does not merit ridicule. With various refinements, the line has many supporters, though that is not sufficient to rule out justified derision; there is nothing so absurd that some philosophers have not expounded it.

What goes on when people sincerely maintain that torture is always wrong, that love is good – or that the knave was right to steal the tarts? Let us glide gently into the topic.

When certain students would ask my views on their essays, I would respond, 'Well, the handwriting is neat.' The statement was factually correct, but I conveyed something more important – that the contents included errors. I may also have been expressing a feeling of despair at their mistakes or my inadequate teaching. 'There's a tarantula' may correctly describe the local world – there really is a tarantula – yet it also spreads fear, panic and desires to be elsewhere.

In moral judgements, the moral element, it is proposed, is nothing more than emotive outbursting. The theory is emotivism or expressivism; it is a species of non-cognitivism, of non-realism: there are no moral properties or facts to cognize, nothing about which to have true or false beliefs. When people assert that actions are right or wrong, good or bad, the moral terms manifest expressions of approval or disapproval. In print, the moral terms could be exclamation marks; different types of marks would represent differences in emotional outburst. The terms, some say, lack literal meaning. More accurately, the terms lack literal meaning if meaning requires worldly features, not merely speakers' attitudes. Of course, when two people disagree morally, factual disagreement appears to be present. Consider the following:

> Benjamin is on a life-support machine, in an apparent persist-ent vegetative state. Jocasta says, 'Turning off his life support is wrong.' Jemima disagrees, 'Turning off is what we must do.' The disagreement may derive from uncertainty of the empir-ical facts. Is he in pain? Is he likely to get better? J and J may, though, be agreed on the facts, yet disagree strongly over the morality of the switch-off. What constitutes that remaining disagreement?

For cognitivists, as ethical realists, the disagreement may be whether Benjamin's life's continuance possesses the property of goodness, whether the switch-off possesses the property of rightness. The utilitarian – a cognitivist – would understand the disagreement as which outcome would maximize happiness. A religious believer, also thereby a cognitivist, may understand the disagreement as which of the alternatives accords with God's will.

Non-cognitivists – emotivists – in contrast, insist that J and J's moral disagreement is one of emotion, attitude or similar, and nothing more. One has the 'hurrah' attitude or expression towards stopping the machine; the other has a 'boo' attitude or expression. That quick caricature of one type of non-cognitivism shows why it is termed 'emotivism', 'expressivism', even the 'boo-hurrah' theory. Moral assertions, understood properly, are no assertions of fact, though it is a fact that the speakers possess the emotions. Emotive outbursts are no more true or false than are yawns and flushes of embarrassment – and expressions 'hurrah' and 'ugh'. When someone shrieks in pain, the shriek is neither true nor false; the shriek expresses pain. When people assert murder to be morally wrong, they are metaphorically just shouting 'boo' at murder.

Spreading ourselves onto the world

Pure emotivists, as said, insist that the moral contents of judgements are nothing but emotional expressions. If, in making moral judgements, we are in part stating that there are certain worldly moral facts, then we are in error. The 'error theory' of morality is that our moral judgements do involve just that mistake; we are unwittingly projecting or spreading our attitudes onto pieces of the world. Compare with how we describe the weather as gloomy: it is we who are gloomy, not the weather; the weather does not feel gloom.

'Spreading ourselves onto the world' is Hume's expression.

WHERE LIVES MORALITY?

David Hume (1711–76), educated at Edinburgh University, is a major Enlightenment figure, awaking Kant from his dogmatic slumbers. Hume understood morality in terms of feelings or sentiments:

> Take any action allowed to be vicious: Wilful murder, for instance. Examine it in all lights, and see if you can find that matter of fact, or real existence, which you call vice… You never can find it, till you turn your reflection into your own breast, and find a sentiment of disapprobation. Here is a fact; but it is the object of feeling, not reason. It lies in yourself, not in the object.

Bertrand Russell (1872–1970), Cambridge mathematician then philosopher, was radical and controversial. In 1916 he was imprisoned for his pacifism, in 1942 sacked from his New York post because of his liberal views on sex. He worked in the tradition of Hume and Mill, was impressed by G. E. Moore and Maynard Keynes. His writings cover numerous topics – many erudite, many popular. Scattered within is anticipation of the 'error theory' of morality:

> There seems to me no doubt that our ethical judgements claim objectivity; but this claim, to my mind, makes them all false… We have emotions of approval and disapproval. If A, B, C, are the things towards which we have emotions of approval, we mistake the similarity of our emotions in the presence of A, B, C… for perception of a common property of A, B, C.

Russell, ever creative, also gave an early version of emotivism:

> When a man says 'this is good in itself', he seems to be making a statement, just as much as if he had said 'this is square.' I believe this to be a mistake… what the man means is: 'I wish everybody to desire this', or 'Would that everybody desired this'.

In 1950, Russell received the Nobel Prize in Literature for his humanitarianism. Later, he helped found the Campaign for Nuclear Disarmament and was imprisoned again for civil disobedience. Up to his death, aged 97, he was still active, issuing political statements.

When we describe events as causes, no metaphysical magnetism or glue exists to bring about the causes' effects; rather, we spread onto the world our expectations of the 'effect' events. Objectively, there are just events following events. When we ascribe goodness or badness to worldly elements – rightness or wrongness to actions – we are, says Hume, 'gilding and staining natural objects with the colours borrowed from internal sentiment'. We may imply moral properties exist 'out there' – but they do not.

Pure emotivism has received modifications: perhaps moral evaluations are disguised imperatives, directives or exclamations of wishes. Telling children that stealing is wrong is ordering them not to steal – or perhaps expressing hopes that they will not.

Some emotivists argue that moral judgements do not solely express emotions but instead, or also, report that the judger possesses the emotions, attitudes or wishes. Thus, an element of subjectivism is introduced: moral judgements assert something true or false about the subject. Let us explore that position, starting with some non-moral subjectivism.

When Ginny insists that gin is nice, she expresses her love for gin; she may also be taken to be reporting something true, namely, that she loves gin, she feels pro-gin. When someone else says that gin is nasty, he is in part saying that he hates gin. They are not disagreeing about gin's properties, but talking at cross-purposes. Moore pointed to that cross-purpose consequence for morality:

> *If*, when one man says, 'This action is right,' and another answers, 'No, it is not right,' with each of them always merely making an assertion about his own feelings, then it plainly follows that there is never really any difference of opinion between them: the one of them is never really contradicting what the other is asserting. And surely, the fact that it involves this consequence is sufficient to condemn it. When I assert an action to be wrong and another man asserts it to be right, he sometimes is denying the very thing which I am asserting.

Whether moral judgements are statements of the speakers' feelings or just expressions of those feelings, one person's moral position is not then contradicting another's. There is no contradiction in people having different feelings. Perhaps, though, morality really does lack space for factual disputes, for formal contradictions; so, let us turn to emotivism's other (seeming) deficiencies.

Emotions – good and bad

We approve and disapprove of things for a range of reasons, many with no explicit moral element. We may be horrified at someone not washing their hands before eating, remaining seated when the Queen enters or wearing socks with sandals; we may say 'hurrah' when the chocolate arrives or even more so the champagne. *Moral* outbursts, it is said, concern matters we care deeply about; but, of course, we also care a lot about many things – not least the champagne. So, even if strong emotions – approvals and disapprovals – are associated with moral pronouncements, such pronouncements must involve something more to make them distinctively moral.

Similar problems apply to versions of the theory that emphasize moral claims as imperatives: my ordering you to hand over the money may or may not relate to morality. Further, regarding the 'imperative' versions: yes, to say that a proposed action is right does possess a prescriptive element – you *ought* to perform it – but to say that a woman is a good woman does not possess any obvious prescriptive element; you may admire that woman without thinking you ought to copy her behaviour.

Emotivists need to separate moral expressions from the non-moral, yet they ought not to propose distinctive moral properties. That would undermine the emotivists' central claim. It is doubtful, in any case, whether any experiences exist that possess a distinctively moral 'feel'. Similarly, it is doubtful whether emotivists can point to any distinctive moral aura possessed by any reasons they give to justify their moral 'boo's and 'hurrah's.

In moral discourse, we seek to convince others to adopt the same beliefs or, in emotivist terms, the same attitudes, emotions or feelings. With many attitudes, emotions and feelings, though, we lack the urge to convert. One person finds sweet drinks disgusting to taste; another does not. We accept such differences; we do not determinedly seek to change minds or tastes – though, true, we may avoid diners who live on hamburgers and beat music. Contrast with moral attitudes: there is no shrug of the shoulders if others, disagreeing with us, maintain that torture, child abuse or theft is good. We recoil. 'You really ought not to do that. Don't you see? That is just wrong, deeply wrong.'

The conversion feature, though, is not sufficient to separate moral from non-moral expressions. We may seek to convert, to persuade others to see the artistic merit of a Rothko painting or to take a certain flight to New York – or to desist from gazing at their mobile phone while at dinner. It could be replied, though, that in those conversion cases, there are moral elements, concerning flourishing or courtesy – some argue for moral dimensions to the arts – in contrast to mere tastes regarding gin.

The above, though, may encourage the thought that no sharp dividing line exists between moral and non-moral concerns: perhaps the moral are at one end of a spectrum of degree of concern. Morality is a matter of taste, but exceptionally strong taste; there is an overwhelming distaste for murder compared with the lighter distaste for dropping litter and not covering the mouth when yawning. Can we, though, take moral judgements sufficiently seriously if they are, at heart, nothing but emotional expressions of taste, albeit with a conversional gloss? We could raise a Moore-type open question objection: what is the explanation of why *those* feelings are so important, needing to be spread? Do we not need *moral* justifications – not ones grounded merely in feelings or emotions – to provide adequate replies?

Turning to moral reasoning, we deploy arguments, find common ground and reach conclusions. Emotivism, as a result, meets trouble – because of a challenge derived from the German logician Frege, later espoused by the twentieth-century philosopher Peter Geach. We start with some benign non-moral reasoning, of the valid form *modus ponens*:

If Miriam wears denim, she will not be admitted.

Miriam wears denim.

Therefore, Miriam will not be admitted.

By parity of reasoning, argues Geach, we should, it seems, accept the following argument as valid:

If Miriam ignored the beggar, then she did something wrong.

Miriam ignored the beggar.

Therefore, Miriam did something wrong.

Such arguments rely on premises and conclusions possessing truth values, with the terms being used consistently throughout. In the moral argument, though, the conclusion for emotivists is equivalent to 'boo' – something without a truth value. Further, the first premise is: *if* Miriam did something, then – well, an expressive 'boo' follows. Can a 'boo' be a conditional 'boo', and could the conditional have a truth value? After all, a pain cannot be a conditional pain. Maybe ways can be found around the problems, but emotivists struggle with this Frege-Geach point of logic.

Here is the biggest problem for emotivism. If morality is constituted solely by expressions of emotions or attitudes – or the issuing of commands or wishes – then what is good and bad would cease to exist if we lacked the relevant emotions, attitudes, wishes or dispositions to command. Many cannot stomach that conclusion. Suppose human emotions underwent dramatic changes such that people delighted in torturing cats and dogs – chimps and children – with yelps of 'hurrah'. That behaviour, *surely*, would still be morally bad. We should be reluctant to read that 'surely' as merely our current expressions of horror. We are more likely to argue: it is because of the moral properties of certain acts that we approve or disapprove of them, have emotions concerning them and seek to show others the true state of moral affairs.

Were we to accept that moral features of moral claims are nothing but emotional expressions, feelings, why should we even contemplate morality as in some way obligatory? Why take it seriously? Emotivism, or any theory of morality as projections of feelings onto the world – the projectionist project – runs the danger of a commitment, somewhere along the line, to, 'If we think it is right then it is right'. Yet, thinking does not usually make things so – and 'attituding' or emoting does not usually make actions right or wrong. Expressions of horror at torture are not what make torture wrong. There are, though, improvements on emotivism – quasi-realism, for example – which aim to avoid the ultimate commitment just mentioned; but it is difficult to see how they can be successful if the grounding must in the end be our current feelings.

For those who argue against morality's objectivity, it is worth noting that we would still possess dispositions, desires and reasons concerning values whether or not the values are deemed objective. I may want to help someone; I therefore have reason to perform that action. There is no need to anguish whether such altruism possesses objective value. There is no reason to think that, if there is no objectivity to moral valuations, self-interest must then be the rational way. Why would that conclusion follow? Whether moral valuations are objective or not, some will still give rational priority to self-interest, whereas others will not. Whether moral valuations are objective or not, we should still criticise someone for being petulant, haughty or uncaring; we should still admire those who bravely stand up against oppression. Even so, many long to know whether there is any objectivity to morality, so let us look afresh at the question.

Despite the arguments against emotivism and its variants, people often remain unconvinced that there can be objective moral properties. They no doubt have the model of such properties being akin to physical properties yet without the physicality. Were moral properties to exist, they would therefore be exceedingly odd, weird, queer and lacking scientific support. Perhaps, though, that is too quick a dismissal. His bank balance is healthy; she is dreaming of unicorns; those politicians broke their promises – such can be objective truths, yet not all the concepts deployed occur in physical theories.

Yes, moral properties – if not identical with natural properties – would be highly distinctive, not least because that an action possesses the property of being right typically indicates what we ought to do, without, of course, causing us to do it. Mathematical properties, though, are also distinctive – and objective – but there is no scientific discovery of numbers; numbers are not causes. Such examples should encourage a less blinkered understanding of objectivity. Many people – and certainly many mathematicians – believe in the objectivity of mathematics, yet we cannot touch the number five or draw perfect right-angled triangles. Maybe, indeed, a proper understanding of objectivity needs no essential reference to objects.

Let us reflect further. Substantial puzzles persist about consciousness and its relationship to neurology, to the physical in general. Grass is green, we say, yet there lurks a perplexing interplay between colour sensations and external reality. Classically, does a tree falling cause a noise, if no sentient beings hear it? If worries about morality's objectivity are of that order, then they are no worse than worries about the objective existence of mountains and oceans, of grass being green and falling trees crashing. Our experiences of colours and sounds, of melodies and movement, must also count as weird and queer, as must the passage of time, the past and the future – if things are deemed normal and 'unweird' only if completely understandable through physics.

Russell wrote, 'It is obvious that a man who can see knows things which a blind man cannot know; but a blind man can know the whole of physics.' There is knowledge that other men have, and the blind man has not, that yet forms no part of physics. So, too, the morally sensitive may possess knowledge that others lack; they possess knowledge that forms no part of science. That is not, of course, to say that what is morally the right action can be determined in the way in which we determine the date and time of the next eclipse of the Sun.

Eclectic ethics; muddled morality

Earlier chapters drew attention to moral features that we readily acknowledge. Morality – the good ship morality – has on board a mishmash of cargoes and a motley crew. Moral matters arise through human welfare, fair distributions, rights and duties, loyalties yet impartialities, flourishing lives, autonomy, love, courage, benevolence, self-restraint, promise-keeping, shame, remorse, admiration, justice, mercy, dignity, forgiveness, magnanimity – and many more and, indeed, much more. Those are values most people recognize as significant when judging what is good and what is right.

The motley crew typically acknowledge the values above, but often come into conflict about how to prioritize them. Children learn swiftly what counts as fairness, and they value it – yet soon disagree about quite what constitutes fair distributions. We readily make appeals such as, 'But how would you feel if I did that to you?' We argue about whether, in particular cases, fairness, say, trumps loyalty to friends or whether, despite the justice of the

HUCKLEBERRY FINN – AND CONSCIENCE

Samuel Clemens (1835–1910), of great fame in his later years as Mark Twain, would dress in a freshly laundered white suit, strolling Fifth Avenue, New York, pleased at churchgoers' awe in seeing the celebrity author Mark Twain pass by. He was, though, an outspoken atheist, outraged at religion's threats of Hell.

Adventures of Huckleberry Finn, recognized as a great American novel, was banned for its coarseness and controversial for its alleged racism, yet curiously, one time, for its anti-racism; either way, it remains popular. Huck is helping his friend Jim to escape slavery. They are going down the Mississippi River, nearing a border and freedom for Jim. Jim is shaking, feverish, so close to freedom. Huck reported:

> Well, I can tell you it made me all over trembly and feverish, too, to hear him, because I begun to get it through my head that he was most free – and who was to blame for that? Why, me. I couldn't get that out of my conscience, no how nor no way… I tried to make out to myself that I warn't to blame, because I didn't run Jim off from his rightful owner; but it warn't no use, conscience up and say, every time: 'But you knowed he was running for his freedom, and you could a paddled ashore and told somebody.' That was so – I couldn't get around that, no way. That was where it pinched.

Doing what is right: Huck was stealing Miss Watson's property; Jim was her slave. Huck's conscience convinced him he was doing wrong, was acting against the law. He was weak-willed in not obeying his conscience; instead, he was yielding to feelings of friendship and sympathy.

Kant stressed rationality, not biological urges, for determining what is right; yet rationality or the Bible led many people – Huck, for example – to think slavery was justified. Many moralists urge obeying one's conscience. Had Huck obeyed *his* conscience, Jim would have been returned to slavery. We surely need serious regard for fellow-feeling, overriding such 'conscience', to live the good life.

punishment, we ought to show mercy. Hospital ethics committees have internal battles: how deep must patient consent really
be, before the vital medical research may be undertaken? With
resources limited, how do we weigh benefits of shorter emergency
ambulance call-out times, thus saving lives, against funding for
IVF treatments that create lives?

With such a motley crew and cargo, it is unsurprising that a
particular moral theory, focusing on one concept or a few, struggles to give voice to others. It is also unsurprising that moral
dilemmas arise – with lapses into moral scepticism. Our starting
point, though, has to be particular cases recognized as morally
significant, where the morality is self-evident; we gave some in
Chapter One. There is no good reason to think, though, that all
cases can be regimented to fit one moral theory. Feet are all feet,
but there is neither one shoe size that fits all, nor one shoe type
that serves for all weathers. Morality, to continue with the analogy,
is not confined to a single garb; sometimes shoes are the priority,
at other times, hats. Sometimes we take the detached perspective
of the universe – for example, greatest happiness – at other times
the personal, attached agent-central perspective of 'I must be loyal'.

In accepting moral values, of cases of right and wrong, good and
bad – and not as mere emotional expressions – we are not thereby
committed to the peculiar features often suggested of moral duty,
namely that moral duty is always overriding, applying universally
in the same way to one and all, with every dilemma possessed of
a correct answer. Yes, on many occasions, often with reflection,
we know what, morally, we ought to do. In many cases, though,
genuine moral conflicts, dilemmas, arise. Dilemmas may be such
that whatever we do, we shall be doing something wrong – yet
in taking one path, we may at least also be doing something right.
The rightness should not be seen as cancelling out the fact that
we are still doing something wrong. If a label is required for the
position advocated here, let it be 'eclectic ethics' or, more down
to earth, 'muddled morality'.

What to say to Hitlers

What may we say to the immoralist, someone who chooses immorality, or to the amoralist who stands aloof of the moral/immoral dimension? What may we say to sceptics who deny the very existence of values? What is there to say to a Hitler – in whichever form he, or she, takes – or to members of the Mafia, the Chinese Triads, or, indeed, al-Shabab and Boko Haram?

G. E. Moore, when addressing philosophers sceptical of a world outside our sense experiences, gave a common sense reply: we are surely more certain that the world contains trees and oceans, independently of us, than we are of the soundness of the sceptics' arguments. Now, Russell commented that common sense is the metaphysics of the Stone Age. Common sense has often been corrected – once it was common sense that the Sun orbited the Earth – yet however radical the scientific discoveries, they have not shown that mountains and trees, knives and forks do not exist; they have not proved that scientists' monitoring devices, which lead to the weird physical theories, lack existence.

In the spirit of Moore, we may have greater confidence in our belief that it is morally wrong to torture children for sheer fun, or to let down a friend on a whim, than in any argument's soundness to the conclusion that it is always fine to go ahead with those deeds. We are more confident that it is wrong to seek to exterminate the Jews – or partake in any genocide – than that any arguments for opposite conclusions are sound. Similar comments apply to the horrors dished out by the Mafia, Triads and, indeed, the opposing forces in Syria, Libya, Iraq *et al.*

The above consideration does not mean that no one would ever delight and think it right to torture children or exterminate a race. Deviances occur. It is natural for frogs to be four-legged, but some three-legged frogs exist, deformed from birth or from unlucky environmental impingings. Humans possess awareness of moral values, but that fails to ensure the absence of corrupt cases, of Hitlers. Even with the Hitlers and the morally disreputable, though, there can be some minimal common ground that could provide a foothold for moral improvement. Thieves maintain honour among thieves; they may be led, through appeals to consistency, to widen their moral appreciation. They may come to see matters in a new light.

A very general point needs making. Should an inability to open the eyes of some people to the moral light, to generate moral sensitivities in them, undermine morality? The answer is 'no'. Consider a different arena: we can be at a loss regarding what to say to those who fail to see how 'Socrates is mortal' logically follows from 'All men are mortal; and Socrates is a man'; yet that does not undermine the validity of such logical deductions. Somewhere along the line, we rely on people just seeing that such a basic argument is a good argument, or that something counts as good evidence for a belief. At some point, nothing more can be said. Why should ethics be any different?

That retort is too quick if applying to moral *theories*: disagreements between utilitarians, deontologists and virtue ethicists are not best understood as some groups having eyes closed, 'just not getting it'. The retort, though, is to the point when considering some clear *cases* of moral values and of immoral and moral behaviour: recall the hound owner and the helpful woman in Chapter One (pp. 3-4). No one should seriously dispute those. If someone cannot see, or refuses to see, that we ought not to torture people against their will, for fun – that we ought not to set ravenous hounds onto children; that we ought not to drive away if having knocked down a pedestrian – and persists in that position despite our appeals and considerations of related examples, then at some point nothing more can be said. Nothing more can be said at all.

♈

There can be the feeling that morality, if well-founded, must be so very compelling that people cannot but act accordingly. 'You *must* not do that.' The imperative, the 'must' – if applicable and understood – ought surely to put a stop to anyone performing the deed in question. If it is true that there must be a prime number between fourteen and eighteen, then there is indeed a prime number located thus. The moral 'must', though, is not like that; it does not coerce. If true that the prisoners must be released, the officers may yet choose not to release.

The moral 'must' is no hurricane destroying all immoralities in its way. There is no magical moral power to be found, if only we searched more diligently. The moral 'must' cannot prevent atrocities being committed in the name of power, politics or religion. The moral 'must' cannot prevent the Hitlers of the world.

Only we can do that.

8

Applying ethics: life and death dilemmas

Most people reading this book have been untouched by moral dilemmas in which life and limbs were at risk. Most people reading this book will not meet life-threatening moral dilemmas involving trams. That certainly is so, assuming typical perception of morality's demands. Readers are unlikely to have been in civil wars, forced to choose between killing innocent villagers and being shot themselves, or, under dictatorships, deciding whether to protest or merely to bind protestors' wounds, either way running the risk of torture. That is not to say we are not exposed to serious moral dilemmas – but they are unlikely to endanger our lives. Our serious moral dilemmas may be very personal; they may concern marital fidelity, kidney donation or assisting elderly parents, suffering pain and indignity, to die.

Serious moral dilemmas also arise on the bigger stage: should you whistle-blow, exposing your employers' supply of arms to repressive regimes, yet risking the jobs of your colleagues? A business that benefits from this country's infrastructure, stability and services, can avoid paying tax by registering as overseas; should it do so? In self-defence, ought a government to authorize the bombing of terrorists operating outside its borders, despite knowing numerous innocent civilians will be maimed or killed? A French humanitarian aid worker, in war-torn lands, is held hostage, threatened with torture and death: are the French authorities right secretly to pay the ransom, despite their international stance against yielding to such demands? Even if the authorities ought not to pay, may it still be right for friends of the worker to do so, if they could raise the funds? Recall the moral differences brought about by agency and relationships (first met through 'Jim and the Indians', p. 36).

As well as big dilemmas, there are, of course, numerous small. The down-and-out on the pavement asks for money; we walk on by, yet should we? We can leave the restaurant without paying for the wine – they forgot to charge us – ought we to tell the staff? A drawing is being sold as junk, as virtually worthless, yet you recognize it as probably a Titian. Should you take advantage of the vendor's ignorance? There is a water shortage; but you want to water your lawn and no one will notice – should you go ahead?

Reflection on morality may open eyes to further moral dilemmas that we – perhaps too conveniently – tend to overlook. Wealthy people often see no immorality in bequeathing assets to their children, yet know that unknown others are in desperate need of financial help whereas their children are not. Finance executives, professional footballers, celebrities, accept remunerations worth millions; do they really deserve such sums when the unemployed and vital workers – nurses, cleaners, shop staff – receive proportionately so very little?

We have argued that people do not always act in self-interested ways; it is true, though, that our overwhelming concern is usually for ourselves, family and close friends. Doubtful considerations are often provided to justify such focus, such self-interest.

> A gift from us to the overseas charity for the impoverished would make only a negligible difference – if the money even reaches the intended people – so it is pointless to give.

Is that true? No doubt money gets wasted, even diverted, but it is likely some lives would still be saved or radically eased. Perhaps we could help in other ways.

Knowing that people are starving to death abroad – and doing nothing about it – is not at all the same as killing them ourselves.

There are differences, but are they morally relevant? Were there a child, desperate for food, in front of you right now, would you not help? If so, why should distance – geography – make so much, or indeed any, moral difference?

I can walk on by, forgetting about the beggars, forgetting about the poor elsewhere, because someone else will help.

Yet should you be the sort of person who leaves any help to others? Is that how you ought to be? What if everyone thought in such a way? Perhaps, in some circumstances, everyone does.

If this country does not supply the weapons to the war-torn regions, others will – so we may as well accept the business, increasing our country's prosperity.

But do we want to live in a country that prospers through aiding others to torture, repress and harm? Is that really a community we should value – a community in which we want to live?

Arguing about abortion

Reason, it is often insisted, has no role in morality; people have moral beliefs grounded in their feelings or in religion – and that is that. This chapter displays some appropriate reasoning in certain life and death controversies, starting with abortion, to reveal underlying principles and potential inconsistencies. Minds may not change, but at least the unchanged minds will better grasp their moral commitments. Sometimes, of course, minds do change.

Abortion is opposed by millions of people with the firm

assertion, 'Life is sacred'. Splendidly sounding as that is, more needs to be said. Perhaps the underlying principle is:

P1. The intentional killing of a life is always morally wrong.

We simply add:

P2. Abortion is the intentional killing of a life.

It follows that – the conclusion is –

C. Abortion is morally wrong.

We have a valid argument: the conclusion C follows from the premisses P1 and P2. Before we accept the conclusion, we need to know whether the premisses are true. Many abortions occur spontaneously, unintended; many occur in non-human animals. Premiss 2 abortions are meant to be those of the intentional killing of a human life. Let us hereafter read Premiss 2 as true by definition, restricted to intended human abortions.

Premiss 1 is easily challenged. Premiss 1 is rarely accepted, even by those who aver that life is sacred. Millions find nothing wrong with killing non-human animals; vegans rarely object to killing mosquitoes, tsetse flies, and weeds of the garden. Premiss 1 minimally needs restriction to human life; even then, few people truly accept that premiss. Many opposed to abortion favour the death penalty and support wars in which innocent civilians are killed. Even if we think of abortion as the killing of innocent life, the killing may be judged collateral damage resulting from the pregnant woman protecting her way of living. Perhaps Premiss 1 needs to be:

P1$_1$ The intentional killing of innocent human life, where the beneficial results do not outweigh the harm of the killing, is morally wrong.

P2 cannot combine with P1$_1$ to justify the required conclusion, for some abortions do lead to outweighing beneficial results for the women; yet many people still oppose those abortions. Their morality is deontological, akin to Kant's: some acts are just wrong, regardless of consequences. Interestingly, when contemplating wars with innocent civilian deaths, those same people often embrace, apparently inconsistently, a consequentialist stance; desirable consequences, such as regime change, receive top priority. The distinction between foreseeing and intending deaths, as earlier found in the Doctrine of Double Effect (p. 58), sometimes shields them from the inconsistency charge: the abortions are intended, but the civilian deaths are merely foreseen.

Let us place the caveat about beneficial consequences to one side and raise a distinct problem with P1$_1$: its focus on human life, its seeming speciesism. What justifies the need for protecting humans when most people accept that non-humans may be killed? That differential treatment seems inconsistent.

The inconsistency is denied. Humans typically possess a feature that (most) non-human animals lack: that is, most humans possess a reflective sense of themselves persisting into the future; they are *persons*. Human beings suffering extreme Alzheimer's, if no longer with a sense of self, on this understanding lack personhood. Persons can reason (even if badly) about their interests. Until now, we have been using 'person' and 'human being' more or less interchangeably, not least because the person/human distinction is drawn in different ways. The distinction, though, one way or another, has moral force – well, so it is claimed. On the one hand, utilitarians could argue that the pleasures of self-aware, persisting individuals with a sense of the future – persons – are greater, or higher, than the immediate pleasures of non-persons. On the other hand, non-utilitarian thinkers, such as Kant, confine moral engagements to creatures with a sense of right and wrong, requiring a sense of self, thus ruling out non-human animals.

Using the person/human distinction, Premiss 1's principle needs to be understood as:

P1$_2$ The intentional killing of innocent persons is morally wrong.

To conclude that abortion is wrong, Premiss 2 would need now to propose that abortion is the intentional killing of persons. Abortion, though, is not that. The foetus must surely be placed on the side of the duck and lamb with regard to awareness, with indeed radically less consciousness, if any at all. No doubt it is wrong to cause a human foetus – duck or lamb – pain, but the painless death of those lives falls, it seems, within the same category. Further, just because the foetus at some stages may experience pain is insufficient reason for rejecting abortions; anaesthesia could be deployed. In any case, the distress of women with unwanted pregnancies easily outweighs any brief foetal pains. It is the killing that is morally challenging.

Religious believers may respond that conception, or some early developmental point, marks the presence of a soul. As there is no biological evidence for a foetus being en-souled, their belief must rest on scripture or be grasped as self-evidently true. Many non-religious believers, though, consider abortion typically to be morally wrong – so let us press on, to see if there are consistent non-religious considerations upholding an anti-abortion stance.

Potentiality may now come to the fore. Only the human foetus possesses the potential to be a person; thus, human abortions are morally wrong. Here we meet obscurity. A potential X is not an X. Acorns are not oak trees; living humans should not be treated as corpses. If invited to dine on chicken, disappointment sets in if served omelettes made from fertilized eggs. Talk of potentiality could be understood as indicating that human abortions are usually preventing persons (developed humans) from entering existence. If we value persons, then it is morally

VOLUNTARY EUTHANASIA: A SLIPPERY SLOPE?

Moral prohibitions sometimes rest on the cry 'slippery slope', a cry often heard over assisted dying – people needing help to end their lives – and voluntary euthanasia, people being killed in their own interests at their request. Permitting either, we shall slide down a slope into accepting forms of involuntary euthanasia – or shall we? Physician-assisted suicide has been legal for years in the US state of Oregon and a few other places, yet with no obvious sliding.

Squares, logical connections: If drawing a square, it logically follows that you are drawing – 'sliding' into drawing – a four-sided figure; but if permitted to read philosophy, that does not slide into enforced philosophy-reading. The voluntary is logically distinct from the involuntary. No slide is justified as a matter of logic.

Sheep, empirical slopes: Logic does not show that a sheep must follow the sheep; but the empirical world is such that a sheep is likely, sheepishly, to follow others. If you have a beer, logic does not dictate you having another; but, as a matter of empirical fact, some slide from sensible drinking to intoxication and drunkenness – just as one chocolate can lead to chocolates too far.

Voluntary sexual intercourse: Acceptance of voluntary sexual intercourse does not entail acceptance of rape. No one argues that voluntary intercourse should be prohibited because we may slide into permitting involuntary intercourse. We encourage awareness of relevant distinctions through education, laws and possible punishments.

Voluntary euthanasia: Opponents need to explain why sliding dangers, if they exist, outweigh the involuntary sufferings many undergo, when unable to end their lives. Opponents need also to explain why intending to reduce suffering via morphine is often permitted even when death is foreseen as a result. Opponents need further to explain why establishing the true intentions of those seeking help to meet their death is any more difficult than telling whether killers intentionally killed. The law is no stranger to judging intentions and coercions – to handling areas of greyness.

wrong to prevent items developing into persons. Abortions do just that; they prevent future persons. If that is good reasoning, then contraception, even sexual abstinence, may be morally wrong; they can prevent the existence of future persons.

That last conclusion is unjustified, it is replied, because with a fertilized ovum, embryo, foetus, there is a *single* entity, tending to develop into a person. The retort is: why should the 'singleness' of the entity be morally relevant? An ovum and a spermatozoon could be seen as a unity, albeit with space between its parts. If it is wrong to prevent a fertilized ovum from developing into a person, then it is surely wrong to prevent the fertilized ovum from entering existence. True, there can be vague talk of how a fertilized ovum possesses an active principle of unity, whereas the sperm and ovum could have gone their separate ways; but when a fertilized ovum has resulted, clearly the ingredients did not go their separate ways.

In view of the above, can contraception and abortion be rightly treated as morally different – ignoring indirect considerations such as medical dangers and distress? Here is a proposal: the nearer we approach – in time and likelihood – a person entering existence, the greater the wrong in preventing that existence. The limiting case, at the late end of the spectrum, is the person existing; clearly it is then wrong, *prima facie*, to halt his continuation. The limiting case at the early end is sexual abstinence, but were abstinence to be forgone, a person may still not result; conception may not even occur. The degree of wrongness, it is being suggested, depends on the likelihood of the action – abstinence, contraception or abortion – blocking the creation of a person. That points to an epistemic feature: namely, what we are justified in believing will likely result from our action or inaction. That feature may also provide some comfort when seeking to justify our greater care for the lives of nearby others than for those far away.

Numerous instances of unprotected sexual intercourse would not ultimately result in persons; hence, contraception is radically less likely to prevent future persons than late abortions. Further, fertilized ova and embryos can naturally fail to develop. Further still, going ahead with a pregnancy now prevents other persons coming into existence: usually a woman cannot be simultaneously twice pregnant. Indirect factors do, in fact, enter the assessment. Very late abortions could generate a casual attitude to human life, running risks of brutalizing human nature.

Biological development – 'nature' – offers no sharp dividing line showing when prevention of a future person's existence is morally acceptable and when not. In practice, lines need drawing. Although of great significance, pragmatic line-drawing required here is otherwise no different from much line-drawing elsewhere. A speed limit is needed, but whether set at 30 mph or 31or 28 – well, it is a matter of decision. Societies draw lines regarding when young people are deemed capable of consent to sexual intercourse. In Britain and many US states, that line is age sixteen, though we know full well that some younger individuals are capable of giving informed consent just as some older are not.

Many people yearn for the 'black or white', thinking there must be a determinate way of telling whether something is right. Morality, though, breathes in areas of grey. Consider the colour spectrum: red, orange, yellow, green, and so on. Central cases of red clearly differ from those of orange, yet there is no determinate borderline between the two. There are many clear-cut cases of what is right and what is wrong; but regarding the generation of people, we meet grey areas – and we next see further factors contributing to that greyness. Before doing so, it is worth noting that philosophers who deploy the human/person distinction are not arguing that, before deciding how to treat a human being, we must judge whether a person is present. We naturally treat human beings as persons and human babies as developing into persons. There are, though, difficult cases, cases we 'naturally' find difficult, where our inclinations need moral reflection and where right actions may yet be performed in sorrow.

Conflicting rights – from violinist to foetus

We have not yet spoken of the rights of the woman and of the foetus. 'Rights' talk can muddy waters; here the talk is shorthand for intuitions regarding basic moral principles. A woman surely should be free to do with her body as she wants, providing she is not harming innocent others; that is her right. Innocent human beings – or, at the very least, persons – surely ought not to be killed; they have a right to life. Put that simply, we have the question again of whether foetuses are persons; but here is a different line.

The Violinist (a tale sketched in 'What does morality demand?', p. xv) is an influential analogy offered by Judith Jarvis Thomson. Let us pretend the foetus is a person with a right to life. The tale suggests that abortion may still be rightly permissible, and not only when the woman's life is endangered. Indeed, even if that latter danger holds, we need a reason why the mother's life should take priority over that of the foetus. Let us say you are the woman in the hospital. On awaking, you find the man, a violinist (as it transpires), plugged into your system. The man needs special lymphocytes that only your blood supplies. So long as he remains plugged, he is fine; and so are you. Well, so are you – except for the inconvenience. Wherever one goes, the other goes too. The man has a right to life, but does he have a right to your blood supply?

The right to something does not typically entail a right to whatever is required for that something. In particular, the right to life does not guarantee the right to whatever is required for life. You have not granted the violinist the right to your blood supply. He is, so to speak, trespassing; hence, you are under no obligation, in terms of rights, to put up with him. The analogy, though, leads to the exposure of degrees and greyness in what morality demands.

First, whether someone has a right to your body depends on circumstances, on what has been agreed or is reasonable to believe. Did the hospital have a known reputation for using patients in that way? Were you aware of the risks? Secondly, even if there is no question of rights, there are other relevant factors. You ought not to be callous and unkind; you would be, if you stopped the man's intrusion, when his need was just for one day. You would be a saint to put up with him for a lifetime; he should not demand that. After a while, perhaps *he* should voluntarily suggest the unplugging. Morality, one may feel, cannot demand saintliness.

Significant differences exist between the violinist-plugging and pregnancy, but also similarities. Even though we are pretending the foetus is a person, we may now see how pregnancies from rape merit treatments different from those of consensual sex, especially where pregnancies from the latter were initially sought. If a woman insists on her right to remove the trespassing foetus because she has changed her mind, now realizing that pregnancy prevents her easy painting of toenails, we should be appalled; and so too if the sole reason for the abortion is that the pregnancy interferes with a planned ski trip. Mind you, if the woman is that way inclined, maybe she is unlikely to be a suitable parent, perhaps pointing to an abortion being appropriate – or adoption.

Thomson introduced the Minimally Decent Samaritan, some- one who appreciates that morality extends beyond rights to the virtues: for example, to compassion, generosity, courage. It can be wrong to insist on one's rights. In cases of pregnancy – and of the plugged-in violinist – what it is minimally decent to do is not solely a matter of respecting rights, but also a matter of moral character, of preparedness to be kind, to help another fellow creature. A woman may suddenly feel unable to go ahead with a desired pregnancy because the father has absconded; as minimally decent, though, she may appreciate the need for courage, harmon- izing with the tenderness she feels for the being she is carrying.

The value of Thomson's Violinist is to draw us away from the thought that abortion is always immoral or that a woman's right to her body always has absolute priority. Here, as elsewhere, morality troubles us because it presents grey areas, matters of degree, of judgement, of different circumstances. Morality surely does not judge a young victim of rape as callous if she has an abortion. Morality presumably is not so favouring of a woman, greatly and voluntarily pregnant, who suddenly insists on her right to have the foetus removed, without reason. It would be casuistry at the level of sophistry for her to argue that she intends removal, but does not intend the foetus's death, merely foreseeing it.

Staying alive: the survival lottery

Whatever people say, the right to life, even if restricted to persons, is not treated as absolute, as paramount. If we seriously held human life paramount, we should resist climbing mountains, imbibing alcohol and rushing down stairs. We should probably withdraw from perils of love and lust, especially in countries permitting 'honour killings'. Mere existence, although necessary, is hardly sufficient for our fulfilment. We enmesh lives in relationships, intimacies, activities and causes, exposing ourselves to physical, psychological and emotional risk.

Most of us – certainly in Western societies – prioritize high-quality living for ourselves over securing even minimal requirements for the lives of many others. Businesses promote consumerism; they encourage feelings of failure if we lack the latest electronic gadgets or wear clothes out of fashion. Consumerism consumes our attention, putting the dispossessed out of mind. Within wealthy countries such as Britain and the US, a certain number of the elderly, frail and poor die of cold each winter. Were greater help given towards heating costs, their lives would be enhanced; deaths would be fewer. Instead of providing that help, governments spend money elsewhere – building high-speed trains, entertaining guests at receptions or yielding to demands for lower taxation.

Other people's right to life fails to persuade us to help much towards their means for life – unless on our doorstep. Perhaps it should. Perhaps the typical understanding of what morality demands fits too snugly into what is convenient – convenient for us to justify our own luxurious living. Sipping the college sherry, discussing moral nuances while in comfortable armchairs, may not be the best context for assessing what morality requires regarding the suffering of millions. Ethics as an academic subject may risk too much detachment – just as do certain moral theories and certain cultural and religious beliefs.

Focusing solely on our own lives, we are still inconsistent. Consider John Harris's Survival Lottery, derived with or without armchair. Background assumptions are that there is always a short-age of organs for transplant and there is a significant risk that, one day, we shall need a transplant – a kidney, for example – yet none will be available. Current availability rests on various accidents, including accidents of whether the deceased ever consented to donation. Here is the lottery solution.

> Let the names of all healthy people enter the Survival Lottery. Tickets, randomly drawn, determine which healthy individu-als, the 'winners', will be painlessly killed, their organs used for required transplants. One healthy person is a potential donor of a range of organs, so the likelihood of you – of any one of us having our name drawn – is lower than the likelihood that, without the lottery, we shall one day need an organ, yet none be available.

Virtually everyone is repelled by the proposal. True, on the pro-posal, innocent healthy 'winners' lose or 'give up' their lives; but without the lottery, innocent unhealthy people lose their lives because of shortages of available organs. At least the lottery draw is fair. The key objection to the lottery is probably Kantian in spirit. We should be deliberately using lottery winners solely as means to an end; we prefer, it seems, to leave whether we live or die more to the (un)lucky draws of nature.

Remaining within the Kantian spirit, respect is due to persons, to autonomous beings; no one should be forced to donate one of his kidneys. Individuals in persistent vegetative states, with no chance of regaining consciousness, though, could have organs removed, their lives unaffected, for they no longer exist as persons; they are but living shells. Often there is reluctance by relatives, though, to permit use of organs in such circumstances. That could derive from doubts about diagnoses, but perhaps from lingering beliefs or hopes that while a body breathes, a soul is present.

Advocating use of organs from the 'living dead' does not mean anything goes regarding the bodies of those deceased. As noted earlier, a person's interests extend beyond his life. We should typically respect deathbed wishes; we ought not to defile corpses. That does not mean that living organs should be left to wither, not helping others to live. Unless contrary to the deceased's earlier informed wishes, making use of his organs is surely rational, sensible and can be performed with respect. We may yet hesitate over that proposed sensible rationality. Perhaps a person and his biology cannot be separated so easily, even conceptually. 'Life and death' matters can make us morally queasy.

Selecting new people – the saviour child

Creating children is a moral matter – and not just one about who will look after them. Think of the controversies and unease over allowing would-be parents to select their children's gender or to abort foetuses with likely impairment. Whose interests do we have in mind? Consider the following.

A couple's child is desperately ill, in need of bone marrow transplantation. The parents could have another child, a 'saviour child', genetically similar for successful marrow donation. It sounds as if the saviour child will be used, immorally, solely as means to an end. The 'solely' ascription, though, may be mistaken. The sole *motive* for the pregnancy is to help the sibling, but the child once born may still be treated as an end in himself. The creation of

COMMODIFICATION: WHAT CAN MONEY BUY?

Some items, commodities, can rightly be bought and sold. Other items ought not. Children – people – ought not to be traded. Mistreating people as commodities differs from mistreating them as objects. A woman may use men as sexual objects without viewing them as commodities to market. Natural beauties, the Grand Canyon – or buildings, the Great Pyramid of Giza, King's Chapel, Cambridge – are objects, yet we should be appalled at bringing them to market.

Sullying and enhancing: Once such items are viewed as commodities, valued in monetary terms, Oscar Wilde's quip applies: there are those 'who know the price of everything, the value of nothing'.

Money can sully. If Nathan has befriended Lady Ludmilla solely for her wealth, then that casts doubt on his friendship. When parents pay children to 'make friends' with their lonely child; they buy pretence, not friendship. Of course, relationships change. Genuine friendships can develop, thereby continuing without cash calls.

Money can enhance. Although value from working should not be solely monetary, people are not respected if paid badly. The awkward question arises: what counts as 'fair pay'?

The money trail: Zach and Amelia sat the same exams for high-flying employment. Zach gets the job, not because he is wealthier, but because his exam answers were better. Why were they better? He received a better university education, though not because of wealth, but his school grades were better. Why were they better? He attended a better school than Amelia – but surely not because of… wealth? Well, yes. His parents could afford costly superior education for him. Money, not just merit, can be the route to success.

We should be appalled at higher grades awarded, if exam answers arrive with large cheques. Exams should be fair; people should succeed through talent. The mindful wealthy, though, ensure their children are better placed than others. Which merits higher priority: equal educational provision or liberty to buy superior education?

Similar questions arise over medical care, even equality before the law. Defendants who instruct expensive lawyers do so because they believe their cases will be better put than otherwise.

children often results from a motivational mishmash, yet is not thereby morally suspect. Indeed, child creation motives are often absent – alcohol and sexual intoxications may be high – yet the offspring outcome is usually valued.

Marrow donation causes discomfort; assume here that there are no lasting adverse consequences. Moral worries persist. How could parents live with themselves, if not helping their child in need by producing the saviour pregnancy? Yet, how will the saviour child feel when of an age to learn what happened? Had he known, maybe he would have agreed to donate; perhaps now he values having helped his sibling. Or does he feel abused? He could simply be pleased, reflecting that, but for the saviour need, he would not have existed. That latter observation leads to moral puzzles over non-existents, as we shall now see.

Start with women who decide not to bear children. May possible children, possible people, have a moral claim? 'Why did you not create us, providing us life?' The question is absurd. Those children do not come into existence, so there is no one who is directly harmed through non-creation – a thought voiced by Henry Salt, an English social reformer:

> A person who is already in existence may feel that he would rather have lived than not, but he must first have the terra firma of existence to argue from: the moment he begins to argue as if from the abyss of the non-existent, he talks nonsense.

Salt's reflection – for someone to be harmed, that someone must exist – does not undermine would-be parents' concern about future offspring. Before conceiving, a woman may sensibly resist smoking, alcohol and recreational drugs; in line with Mill's thinking, she may also ensure sufficient financial resources. She is being procreatively beneficent.

Consider a couple intent on having a child; they learn that if conception occurs now, the child will be born severely disabled, a lifetime of pain ahead. Perhaps the woman has a genetic disorder. Will they not harm that currently non-existent child by going ahead with the planned family? It would surely be immoral knowingly to create a life of pain; yet if that child is not conceived, there is no child who has been saved from harm. How can a benefit be delivered to a non-existent?

Add the supplement: by waiting three months without conceiving, the woman's disorder is corrected; a conception can then take place, a healthy child resulting. The thought may be:

It would be better for your child if you delay conception.

That is paradoxical. It cannot be better for the child not born, to be born later – for there is no such child. If delay happens, then the (unhealthy) child who would have been conceived is not conceived. Someone else gets conceived and born – according to current biological theory. Conception deferment seems right; but, what wrong would be committed, if the woman went ahead now, giving birth to a distressed child, growing into a suffering adult? Would that be a 'wrongful birth'?

If the non-delayed conception goes ahead, presumably harm rests, in part, on whether the resultant child's life is harmful to him (or others). If he is pleased to be alive, then no overall harm has been done to him; mind you, a healthy child, who would have been conceived three months later, misses out on existence. That missing is no harm, given the reasons of Salt. If, though, the child ends up feeling he would rather not have been born, then he has been harmed. Hence, if the couple decide not to proceed with the conception now, they could be benefiting someone who forever lacks existence, namely the child who would have been born, yet wished he had not. That retains the paradoxical ring.

Ignoring the question, if even sensical, of whether it is better never to have existed – maybe pains in life inevitably outweigh pleasures – there remain questions of the moral permissibility of affecting lives that we do intend to create. Most (would-be) parents seek to influence their offspring, though the outcome may well be disappointing. Some parents prefer a child with lots of siblings; others do not. Some could well elect for interventions, were they possible, to produce children with yens for baseball, others for chess – with blue eyes, others with brown.

Our morality undoubtedly rests with an idea of what minimally constitutes a biologically healthy human life. Most people are appalled at deaf parents who deliberately want their children to be deaf, preventing medical interventions to cure any expected deafness. Such parents argue life for all of them would be better with their children as part of the deaf community. We should resist that argument; it would apparently justify such deaf parents deliberately causing deafness in babies born with good hearing.

Here it is worth noting how conditions that we should avoid may yet, in particular cases, lead to beneficial results. Consider a young, frivolous, aimless man who, because of a bomb blast, loses his legs; as a result of that tragic loss, he becomes determined to make something of his life. After immense effort, he triumphs in the Paralympics; he becomes a model for other people disabled. His life – the view from his 'here and now' – has meaning. He looks back and values, sincerely values, the earlier tragedy; but no one would seriously suggest it is therefore good to blow people's legs off. Return to the woman who, if she conceives now, will bring a disabled child into the world. She goes ahead with the conception. She loves the child; the child grows into an adult, perhaps pleased to have been born – yet we may still rightly believe the conception morally ill-judged.

Typically we support therapy, curing diseases, correcting for genetic defects; yet we may frown upon enhancements designed to take children beyond 'natural' abilities. Perhaps the fear is that a superclass could be created by those sufficiently wealthy to pay for intelligence and beauty enhancements for their offspring. Perhaps the frowning manifests a fear of society with eugenics programmes, permitting only certain types of humans to exist.

Preferences for certain characteristics in offspring can manifest a disrespect for existent individuals lacking those characteristics: consider those who want only sons, aborting daughters, or those who would embrace therapies designed to prevent children from becoming homosexual – or even atheist. Preferences over children's characteristics, though, do not have to imply disrespect for individuals lacking the desired characteristics. To note that everyone would prefer not to be paralysed – and would eagerly have a foetus treated to avoid paralysis when born – does not remotely imply disrespect for paralysed people now existing. Valuing contraception does not imply a low opinion of people who result from contraceptives not being used.

As ever, we seek lines – here lines between morally desirable and undesirable enhancements. As ever, there are smudges rather than lines; after all, it is undoubtedly good to have more or less eradicated smallpox, but would it be good, through foetal enhancements, to eradicate poor mathematical ability, sexual jealousy or melancholy? Of course, such questions bring forth puzzles again of our free will, and how far others should be permitted to determine our character traits, our nature.

♈

Matters of life and death, as just seen, involve the medley of moral concerns, the motley cargo encountered in our review of various moral theories. The topics here have been viewed mainly within the personal realm, but, of course, they are affected by societal surroundings. That raises questions of which interferences are permissible by a state and its laws – and how surroundings, wider still, may morally impinge on us. Morality extends beyond the personal, beyond the community – maybe beyond even those beings who are sentient, to the environment as a whole.

We are about to feel the long arm of morality.

9

No man is an island: from community to ecology

'No man is an island', wrote John Donne – and unless we are to be hermits, isolated, un-impinging one upon the other, we find ourselves within communities, communities that rely upon governments, laws and conventions. We are enmeshed further, within more than our community – be it tribe, nation or state – for we are members of the human race, connected to people further afield through increasing global internet and commodity transmissions. We are enmeshed further still, for we sense responsibilities for future generations – think of worries about global warming – and even regret injustices cast upon generations past. Recently, Britain formally apologized for the torture of Kenyan rebels in the 1950s. Alan Turing, the prime mover in cracking World War II's Enigma Code, received a posthumous royal pardon for his offences against the then anti-homosexuality laws. That is curious – for the need, if any, is to apologize for the existence of those laws that blighted the lives of thousands.

We have confined ourselves, above, to human beings. Over the centuries, the extension of morality possessed mainly human-centred motivations, with reformers embracing those humans once largely outside moral consideration: the barbarians, the slaves, the women. Reformers persuaded opponents to attend more carefully – to see the humanity common to all. Yet our lives interplay with far greater diversity, from non-human mammals, farmed, wild or as pets – to salmon, butterflies and the silver birch – to deserts, cliffs and oceans, indeed, the planet itself. Our moral concern expands, overcoming an anthropological narcissism.

First, we zoom out to the community, the state, assessing how it may morally impinge upon individuals; we then look beyond humanity, to see how wide is morality's embrace.

Passing unwounded – between excess authority and excess liberty

A community imposes itself upon its members through laws, rules and customs. For ease, let us speak mainly of the state and its laws. What moral justification is there for the state possessing power – power to punish lawbreakers?

Morality's presence is exhibited in, for example, common Western thinking that people ought to be allowed to live as they think best without unwarranted intrusions on, and from, others. That already presupposes a feeling that individuals, in some way, merit equal respect – though only 'in some way'. Some Western governments measure society's success in terms of increasing gross domestic product or full employment, or perhaps – with more subtlety – the sense of well-being. Such success, though, may conflict with what is morally desirable. Vast inequalities of wealth, with a labouring class low paid, may increase gross domestic product, even improve living for all. It is exceedingly doubtful whether that latter claim is true, but even if it is, such inequalities strike many as immoral, leaving the very poor powerless, lacking respect, excluded from many of life's goods.

As expressed by Hobbes, the vexing problem is how society can pass unwounded between excess authority and excess liberty. What makes a state's laws morally acceptable – not excessive – such that they merit obedience? A simple response is: people benefit. That fails to show, though, why non-beneficiaries – maybe many at the bottom of society – should keep the law. Even the successful may argue that their benefits from society would be greater, were there fewer laws upholding employment rights and high taxation; they probably overlook their reliance on society's ethos, supportive of private ownership and property rights despite great wealth disparities.

Even when people do secure benefits through living in a stable state of law enforced, it is questionable whether therefore, morally, they should obey the law; after all, the benefits may be unsought. If someone buys me dinner, unrequested by me, I am not thereby under an obligation to return the favour, even if I accept the dinner and enjoy dining. You find the street lighting useful, but if it arrived not at your request, why should you pay towards its cost or obey laws relating to it?

The American Declaration of Independence speaks of governments deriving their just powers from consent of the governed – in line with John Locke's philosophy. Locke reasonably proposed that obedience to the state is justified when through people's voluntary consent: voluntarism. That consent is shown, he unreasonably proposed, by people continuing to live under the law, using the state's facilities and 'walking the King's Highway'. Such consent – tacit consent – is rightly challenged. To leave the home society permanently is no viable option for most people. It would be akin to jumping from a ship into a raging ocean when disagreeing with the captain's orders – a nice example from Hume.

Were the tacit consent criterion successful in justifying obedience, then presence in an atrocious authoritarian or totalitarian state could also demonstrate morally justified obedience. A proposal, to overcome that problem, is that the just state, one that merits obedience, has laws to which all *rational* individuals would voluntarily consent. To live well, people need to cooperate; thus, they must bind themselves via a mutually acceptable 'social

WHAT PRICE LIBERTY?

Western societies prize liberty; yet sometimes the state rightfully – paternalistically – intervenes, protecting people from themselves.

Bringing up children: Should the state prevent parents from feeding children junk food containing excessive salt and sugar, damaging health? Should it be banned, along with alcohol, cannabis and cigarettes? Governments impose restrictions; but which are justified? Adults should be free to decide what to feed their children and consume as they want, argues powerful business. Perhaps, though, the wants are not 'their' wants, but imposed via advertising, turning young and old into avid consumers.

Forced to be free: The phrase is from Jean-Jacques Rousseau. Preventing certain consumers from doing what they want may be freeing them. If they fully grasped the dangers to health, the advertisers' manipulations, they would want to overcome their undesirable desires. State prohibitions would enable them to do just that – namely, not engage in unhealthy living. Businesses, though, with the god of profit, typically denigrate calls for marketing restrictions. They encourage credit and impetuous spending, often wrongly claiming their overriding duty must be to maximize shareholder returns.

Organs for sale: A poor woman wants to auction one of her kidneys. Many Western countries prohibit such sales. The recipient, though, would be benefited, securing a full life ahead. The woman's health may even improve, for she could then afford to eat well and support her family. Organ donation is permitted, so why not organ sale? Similar thoughts apply to free markets in sexual services.

People ought not to be so desperate to need to sell their organs, but their plight is not eased by bans on sales; yet without bans, more of the poor could be tempted to sell. People could become seen as commodities.

Unintended consequences: Laws to help people in general can harm the needy. Minimum wage laws harm those so desperate that they would work for less. Absence of such laws, though, can lead to downward spirals and increasing exploitation of employees. As ever, where should lines be drawn?

contract' that determines the law's basic principles. None of us has made such a contract; so theorists often turn to hypotheticals.

On the one hand, Kantian contractualists focus on what agents could rationally justify to each other. On the other hand, contractarians, following the recent John Rawls, ask us to go behind a 'veil of ignorance'. Let us look at that veil.

Pretend that we are veiled from seeing how things will turn out for us in the resultant society. Behind the veil, we have no idea of our status – whether we are male, Muslim, Jew, talented, disabled, and so forth. I am behind the veil; my aim is to flourish. To what would it be rational to consent? That question may baffle. Yes, it is rational for me to consent to what is best for me, yet what is this 'me' now stripped of my distinctive features, my beliefs about the good life, about likelihoods, and so forth?

At least, goes the argument, it would be rational for me to support laws that allowed people, equally, to be free to choose how to live, providing not harming others. Aware that I may be poor, a cancer sufferer, untalented, in the resultant society, it would be rational to support taxation for provision of education, welfare benefits and equal opportunities. A difference principle, it is controversially suggested, should demand rational assent: that is, wealth inequalities should be permitted only in as far as they make things better for the most disadvantaged.

Thus it is that Rawls sets the basic liberal principles for a just society. Those principles could also be justified, if you asked yourself what sort of society you would wish for, if you knew that your worst enemy would be allocating you your place in that society.

Contractarianism grounded in veiled (that is, ignorant) 'self'-interest is not an obvious grounding for morality, even when restricted solely to justifying laws of the state. Until Carruthers knows he is born talented, healthy and with a silver spoon in his mouth, he rationally consents – behind the veil – to a society providing welfare, educational and other social benefits through heavy taxation. Once in his fortunate position – with the silver spoon – if rational self-interest remains the motive, he would be right to evade taxes, breaking the law when in his interests so to do. In fact, when we break the law, we may experience guilt and remorse; yet if law-breaking is wrong only if endangering self-interest, why should we experience such feelings?

Kantian deontologists, we saw earlier, argued that self-interest could not be a moral motivator; virtue ethicists argued that the truly virtuous would often act in the interests of others. To keep the law solely for our own self-interested benefit hence reaps moral challenge. As with religious aims for bliss eternal through good deeds here on Earth, so too the state's institution of punishment threatens 'good' behaviour's moral status; individuals have the self-interested motive of avoiding punishment – a motive, though, happily accepted and encouraged by utilitarians such as Bentham.

To overcome objections to the self-interest lurking within the 'veil' approach, we should need to consent, when behind the veil, to law-keeping taking priority over self-interest once within society. Arguments are needed, then, to show both why, when behind the veil, the commitment to continual consent would be rational and why, when no longer veiled, that commitment should be maintained. After all, once within society, we may come to hold deep convictions – that God demands chastity before marriage or that land should be in common ownership – convictions so deep that we could not possibly acquiesce in laws promoting sexual liberation or upholding private property and corporate power, laws that appeared rational when ignorantly behind the veil.

Redistribution of eyes?

Rawls's just state is a liberal welfare state, one that derives from respecting people's lives, their autonomy and diversity. The same considerations, manifested in the work of libertarians such as the recent Robert Nozick, lead to a very different state, its sole function being nightwatchman, protecting citizens from intruders.

The Nozickean libertarian reasoning appears simple and convincing. We surely own our bodies. It would be unjust if the state painlessly removed an eye from some two-eyed in order to distribute eyes to the blind. From respect for people and ownership – 'self-ownership' became the curious term of art – we should infer that it is typically wrong to take, to steal, the fruits of people's labour and what they have justly inherited. Compulsory taxation for any reason other than providing for the police, army and judicial services, is stealing; it is akin to treating people as slaves.

Proper to me, it is claimed, are attitudes of respect for my autonomy; I should be at liberty to act as I want, if not harming others. Through ticket purchases and attendances at opera, gigs and sporting events, we voluntary engage in transactions that lead to a talented, charismatic or lucky few becoming vastly wealthier than others. What is wrong with that? Levying taxes in order to redistribute wealth to help the poor violates those taxed.

One way of judging between the liberal and the libertarian stances, briefly outlined, is by assessing consistency. Respecting people's autonomy should not be one-sided. The libertarians' acceptance of wealth inequalities – respecting the wealthy – ignores how such wealth reduces opportunities for, and hence autonomy of, the poor. Private ownership of land, of the coast and forests, restricts people's liberty to wander. Furthermore, taxing, say, transactions that lead to inequalities, to enable improved autonomy for the poor, need not disrespect the wealthy. They are being respected by ensuring that taxation levels do not leave them struggling. Further still, we do not seriously believe that a person's relationship to his liver and kidneys is a good model for grasping his relationship to the parsnips he has grown, the café service he provides or the tips he receives. Talk of body and organs as properly owned, as property, risks seeing them as commodities ready to market; ought we really to see human beings and their parts in that way?

Nozick's libertarianism – even if it can overcome the above criticisms – does not establish that what the wealthy currently own and receive should be untouched by taxation. Nozick objects to violations of justice, arguing for compensation for those affected. Much current wealth and many incomes have derived through *unjust* transactions. Great landowners gained their greatness from kings, queens and dukes, generations ago, taking land by force. Settlers in North America infringed the autonomy of the indigenous, securing wealth they later passed down the settling generations. Thus the current state of affairs typically is not one of just ownership, as understood by Nozick.

If a state – any state – morally merits obedience, then its laws must at least cohere with fundamental moral principles over not harming others. On that, Rawls and Nozick agree. The laws, we may insist, should otherwise be silent on many moral matters, notably those concerning consenting adults in private. Often that silence is morally justified by a liberal and libertarian awareness that there is no one 'right way' for good living. People value different things in life; that pluralism needs to be respected. Behind the veil, rationality would point to laws permitting, even encouraging, in Mill's terms, experiments in living. The state as totalitarian, intruding vastly in citizens' lives, would be infringing the citizens' autonomy, their experiments in living that may concern, for example, the spiritual, sexual or simple material indulgence.

Even if individual liberty standardly takes a very high priority and embraces the idea of just ownership, that does not prevent community interest sometimes superseding. Authorities should have no right to destroy your home; but with the emergency of London's Great Fire raging, they rightly pulled down an innocent man's house against his will in the hope of preventing the flames spreading. Recent floods in Britain led to water diversions, some properties being sacrificed to protect villages elsewhere. Obviously, there are disputed cases: Britain maintains tight gun controls to protect the community, whereas the US vests in individuals 'the right to keep and bear arms' and even allows children the use of guns. Medical ethics committees may baulk at heart attack patients, in no position to consent, being in random trials; some receive adrenalin treatment, others placebos. Results will benefit the community, but some, unwittingly in the trial, may die, having received one treatment rather than the other.

Community interests vie with individual, for example, over the siting of airports, nuclear waste dumps and shelters for the homeless. The inhabitants of Wolfenschiessen, a Swiss village, initially objected to nearby nuclear dumping: the authorities' offer of money was an outrageous bribe; yet gradually the inhabitants viewed it as morally appropriate compensation. What made the difference? One and the same action can be seen differently, as morally different, at different times. Smoking in public was once a welcome freedom of expression; now it is an intrusion upon others, a threat to health, often prohibited in closed public spaces – yet ever amplified loud music, despite its intrusion and harmful effects on hearing and psychology, is permitted, spreading through stores, bars and restaurants, attacking those who seek quiet conversation or even just quiet. Reason would suggest encouragement of diversity – with smoking bars and non-smoking bars, with beat-filled bars and the beatless – yet reason can be scarce.

Toleration: the neutral state as ringmaster

Certain moral principles are required for any state to be just. That may offend both lovers of cultural relativism and lovers of democracy, understood as majoritarian rule or ochlocracy, rule by the mob. Democracies, meriting moral desirability, maintain laws promoting human rights – rights to equality before the law and freedom of expression. Any state, whatever the majority vote,

WHEN THE PRIVATE INTRUDES UPON THE PUBLIC

Burqas, but not bikinis? Safia, a devout Muslim, works in a liberally minded London institution. She cannot, of course, remove her Muslim belief during working hours, so she is granted exemption from the dress code: she may wear her burqa. Sophia, one hot summer's day – such days can occur in London – appears in a bikini. She is threatened with dismissal, as is Sylvester, a transvestite, who insists on wearing frilly dresses, despite his manly beard.

Exemptions are sometimes granted on religious grounds, but not on other. Motorcycling Sikhs in Britain are exempt from wearing helmets, yet nothing in the Sikh religion demands such travel; there are buses, bicycles and feet. Some justify exemptions on the basis of conscience or deep-seated belief. Conscience and belief can, though, deliver support for murder and persecutions. How, then, should exemptions be decided?

Which right trumps? The European Court of Human Rights, in 2014, upheld France's ban on women wearing full-faced veils in public. The Court accepted that such concealments undermine open interpersonal relations and the community value of 'living together', breaching the right of people to live in a 'space of socialisation'. The Muslim woman who wanted the ban lifted said she freely chose to wear the burqa; so her rights to free expression, her conscience and religion, were violated.

Elane Photography: A small New Mexico photographic business, conservative, Christian, declined to photograph same-sex ceremonies. It was found guilty of discrimination, no exemption permitted. The US Supreme Court refused to intervene.

A student rents out rooms in his house, aware that lodging relationships could transform his romantic life. May he advertise for women only, in their twenties and raven-haired? May he advertise solely for black women or Far Eastern? Or is that unfair discrimination?

Discriminations: Many permitted in private are prohibited in public, but on what moral basis? Where does the private end and the public begin? What justifies difference in treatment?

morally should have laws against slavery, against unjust killings and harms – and against imposition of enforced religion.

In any state, there is the question of what constitutes harm. According to some sincerely held beliefs, homosexual practices, contraception and rejection of God are harmful, if only by way of risking eternal damnation. Hence, contrary to any implied respect for pluralism over ways of living well, many believe that there is fundamentally only one way in which people should be allowed to live; there is only one true human flourishing. Totalitarian and theocratic states have that monistic understanding of the good life – a perfectionist stance – in contrast to liberal states and their pluralism. Can monistic claims be properly challenged?

Given clear disagreements about how to live well, the state, it seems, has to be neutral, allowing people to make the best of what they judge the best. The neutral state could be conceived as ringmaster, permitting a diversity of acts, rather than conductor, insisting that all sing from the same hymn sheet. The state is not thereby value neutral; the stately ringmaster ensures, to some degree, that no act intrudes upon another. Unless the permissive laws give rise to harm, recognized by believers and non-believers alike, a neutral state permits abortion, euthanasia and liberty in sexual relations. Many religious believers would be offended, but that distress derives, in part, from their belief – and is very different from harm caused by direct attacks, physical or psychological. At least in the neutral state, the offended possess the freedom to convince others to join their cause.

One complaint is that the neutral state, mainly with laws to prevent harm – to prevent vice rather than encourage virtue – is too minimal for its citizens to flourish. There are, though, degrees and degrees. As well as education and welfare provision, the neutral state may fund arts, sports and healthy eating, encouraging development of abilities and opportunities. The state need not be a necessary evil, but an enabler – enabling people to live their lives, to flourish, at least to some extent, as they would want.

Another complaint is that the neutral state glorifies individualism, rejecting tradition and community values; it leads to a fragmented society, one far from flourishing. The response, once again, points to degree and degree; after all, those who stress tradition and community – communitarians – do not thereby disparage all individual liberty. Our sense of cultural identity – ideas 'furnished from the wardrobe of a moral imagination' said Edmund Burke – can indeed nurture and unite our affections, yet respect for identity and tradition can keep people in their place, oppressing minorities, upholding unjustified discriminations. 'The desire to be in unity with our fellow creatures,' notes Mill, tends 'to become stronger, even without express inculcation, from the influences of advancing civilisation.' Advancement often means jettisoning certain traditions – of sexual inequality, franchise restrictions and enforced religious observance.

Morality's motley cargo, unsurprisingly, includes both individual and community values. They inevitably entwine, sometimes in tension, sometimes in harmony. They need to be assessed, case by case – and reassessed case by case. For example, current calls for sexual equality – equal percentages of men and women in given occupations – may fly in the face of what people want and need to fill their lives. Calls to respect traditions could end up defending female genital mutilation, forced marriages and so-called 'honour killings'.

Generations: future and past

Many people accept the moral desirability of individuals being free to conduct their lives as they want, if not harming others. That is the heart of Mill's Liberty Principle. Which individuals concern us? 'All' – but that answer is glib. These days, we usually accept the interests of all currently living human beings; but many find it difficult to place much weight on the interests of, say, the lobster soon to be boiled alive. We lead up to the lobster – but first, future human beings. Does the moral embrace extend to them?

We may endorse the 'person affecting restriction' as met earlier courtesy of Henry Salt: for benefits or harms to arise, there must be someone who benefits or is harmed. We need have no concern for possible people who could be created, yet will not be created. There are, though, generations, unknown to us; they will exist. For simplicity, we ignore generations overlapping with us.

Future non-overlapping generations do not currently exist; hence, if justice rests upon the possibility of reciprocation, then intergenerational justice, fairness to other generations, is non-existent. We can affect future generations, their numbers and well-being; they cannot affect us. Revising slightly Joseph Addison's observation, 'We are always doing something for Posterity, but I would fain see Posterity doing something for us.'

Justice understood in terms of self-interested reciprocation – contractarianism – has in any case been found wanting; but we may have, instead, a direct moral worry about how current policies affect future generations, be it through global warming, over-fishing or even the size of national debts. That latter anxiety overlooks the infrastructures, medical knowledge, judicial traditions *et al.* readily available to future generations, but non-existent for earlier.

To what extent should we take account of future people's well-being? One answer is: to the extent of not depleting resources so considerably that future generations will be seriously harmed. Earlier generations provided resources for us; we should pass them on in good order. The Earth's resources are under our stewardship. Concern for future generations' well-being, though, runs the danger of reduced concern for today's individuals. We know, without any doubt, of millions suffering right now, but we have no certain knowledge of how life will be in a hundred years' time. A hundred years ago, did many predict the nature and availability of today's resources? Paradoxically, we are far more certain of how things will be for human beings in a billion years' time – namely, their non-existence.

Regarding generations past, they have done a lot for us indirectly, whether wittingly or not. Can we do anything for them? The answer is: yes, though not much. We can show respect for what they did – and regret the numerous injustices that hit so many. Recall the earlier examples of Kenyan rebels and Alan Turing.

Speciesism: liberating non-human animals

It is morally wrong to torture innocent people, to eat them or use them for medical or shampoo experimentation without their consent. That stance is readily accepted. Once non-human animals enter the frame, moral sensibilities radically reduce. Many morally minded people see nothing wrong in eating non-human animals, yet many of those animals, before meeting death, suffer appallingly. The quip that they should therefore welcome death is a quip too far, given our indirect responsibility in causing much of their suffering. Think of boiling lobsters alive. Think of battery farms. Think, too, of bull fights, the ivory trade and, in China, bears reared in tiny cages for their bile.

Animal rights' defenders combat the appalling treatment of non-humans; but others combat the very idea of animal rights. As already seen, rights are sometimes understood as requiring awareness of contracting, reciprocation and duty – awareness that non-humans lack. True, there once were animal trials. Sassetta, in his *Legend of the Wolf of Gubbio*, depicts a wolf agreeing via the good offices of St Francis to cease terrorizing inhabitants; in return he would receive regular food. Defence council for some rats justified their courtly absence by reference to the perils of travelling near their mortal enemies – cats. No one, though, seriously thinks that, in reality, wolves – pigs, rats or even chimps – have awareness of right and wrong. Human babies are in the same boat; so, any contractarian basis of rights heads into the mire of babies' potentialities – touched upon earlier regarding abortion and the human/person distinction. Human babies possess potential for grasp of duties, for developing into persons; non-human animals do not. That is the line, difficult as it is to uphold.

Entering the 'rights' debate regarding non-human animals is to be fishing for red herrings. Let us simply concede that it is morally wrong to harm a whole range of animals, human or otherwise. That wrong, some argue, derives solely from *our* human interests. Kant speaks of our having indirect duties to certain non-human animals; the duties arise because of our direct duties to other people. If we damage animals, we may be damaging someone's property. If we inflict pain on animals, we may be led into mistreating people.

Kant seems guilty of speciesism. Speciesism is often modelled on racism and sexism. Lives ought not to be treated differently unless differences can be morally justified. No sexism is involved in providing cervical cancer screening only to women; but to provide that screening to women for their well-being, but not prostate cancer screening to men for their well-being, would be sexist and unjust – unless relevant probability or curing differences exist. Sexism may be evident, we controversially suggest, in the scant concern for the average male lifespan being shorter than the average female's. There are significant longevity discrepancies between the poor and the rich, yet there is often political opposition to reduction in wealth inequalities, manifesting, we may say, 'wealthism'.

Is speciesism akin to sexism? It would be patronising – sexist, indeed – if women were to decide how men should be treated, or vice versa. Men and women engage in dialogue about their flourishing ways; there is no inter-species dialogue. Humans decide how to treat other species; non-humans do not, and cannot, decide how to treat humans. Numerous features justify differential treatments of different animals; sending llamas to school would be silly. Is there, though, any morally relevant difference that justifies our farming and eating lambs, chickens and geese, but not babies, children and adult humans?

After noting that blackness of skin is no reason to abandon someone to tormentors, Bentham wrote:

> It may one day come to be recognized that the number of legs, the villosity of the skin, or the termination of the os sacrum are reasons equally insufficient for abandoning a sensitive being to the same fate, that of the caprice of a tormentor… The question is not, Can they reason? nor, Can they talk? but, Can they suffer? The time will come when humanity will extend its mantle over everything which breathes.

Despite recognizing that animal suffering is morally relevant, meat-eating utilitarians may play the card of maximizing happiness. Perhaps our carnivore pleasures outweigh the combined sufferings of non-human animals, sufferings necessary for those pleasures, and our own sufferings from increased heart disease. Even were such outweighing to exist – where is the evidence? – we may question its significance. Utilitarian reasoning is usually modified to avoid calculations that would otherwise justify factory-farming human slaves and eating babies of a minority race. To avoid speciesism, similar modifications could be made, ensuring that non-human animal suffering is not treated merely as an uncomfortable means to an overall beneficial end.

It is not because non-human animals are non-human that makes it permissible to kill them – runs a non-speciesist argument – but because they lack personhood (when they do). Individuals – *persons* – with self-awareness, reasoning, conscious of future continuation, of eventual ceasing to be, possess a right to life: that is, it is seriously wrong to kill them. Killing lambs is not thwarting the lambs' sense of a future, for, it is claimed, they lack such sense, though killing chimps, gorillas, dolphins, even crows, may be wrong. Perhaps they are non-human persons in that they do, in some ways, possess a sense of self-persisting, even if no language for expressing it. Many of us would indeed feel uneasy at choosing roast gorilla or dolphin casserole. Many of us do, though, eat pork, despite the apparent intelligence and possible sense of self of pigs.

The argument just given, rather conveniently, justifies current practices of dining on duck and deer, but not on humans; after all, we have no real idea of how the future is, or is not, viewed by ducks and deer. There is little agreement, as demonstrated by the vague characteristics just listed, over quite what constitutes personhood. Maybe the essential point is that, unlike humans, other animals presumably do not reflect on the possibility of death for themselves and for others. Whichever relevant differences do apply, there is no good justification for the suffering caused by some farming practices, cages and abattoirs, be the creatures stunned first – or facing death unstunned, as they often are, for halal and kosher diners.

That non-human animals can suffer and undergo pleasures shows that they have interests, even if they are not persons. Those interests should carry moral weight. That, according to Tom Regan, vindicates animal rights. Animals that are subjects of life and experiences possess inherent value; thus they morally ought not to be used solely as means to an end. Animal experimentation, commercial farming, even sports using animals, are wrongs.

Sometimes wrongs have to be committed for a greater good: killing the pet goat prevents the owner from starvation, though we need reasons why the owner's life takes priority. Generally, argues Regan, deliberately killing experiencing subjects for food is wrong. The response sometimes is that meat-eating may be beneficial to some animals, if – *if* – it results in animals being created, having pleasurable full lives, and then being killed painlessly. We would then be acting in their interests – their pleasures being relevant – and not solely for meat-loving ends.

ITEMS OF VALUE – WITH OR WITHOUT VALUERS?

G. E. Moore (1873–1958) was a major influence on early twentieth-century thought, admired by economist Maynard Keynes, by the Bloomsbury Group and by Cambridge's well-known secret society, The Apostles. Communion with the beautiful, the beloved and truth are the most valuable states. In those days, noted Keynes, social action, wealth, success, were 'less prominent in our philosophy than with St Francis of Assisi, who at least made collections for the birds'.

Moore's Two Worlds: Moore proposed a thought experiment to show that some items possess intrinsic value. Beauty is the value here.

> Let us imagine one world exceedingly beautiful. Imagine it as beautiful as you can; put into it whatever on this earth you most admire – mountains, rivers, the sea; trees, and sunsets, stars and moon. Imagine these all combined in the most exquisite proportions, so that no one thing jars against another, but each contributes to increase the beauty of the whole. And then imagine the ugliest world you can possibly conceive. Imagine it simply one heap of filth, containing everything most disgusting to us, and the whole, as far as may be without one redeeming feature.

Many would claim – as would Sidgwick, the utilitarian encountered earlier – that the question of the worlds' values arises only if human beings are present to contemplate them. Moore disagreed: even if there were no humans present, it is better that the beautiful world should exist, than the ugly. Later, it seems, Moore had a change of heart: intrinsic goods necessarily involve consciousness or feelings.

The fly's perspective: Were we able to adopt such a perspective, we may well place greater value on the ugly world. The descriptions of the two worlds carry human valuations. Suppose the descriptions were in terms of molecular motions: then we should spot no relevant difference between the worlds. That scientific reductionism, it may be replied, omits essential features – colours, textures – that really exist.

Perhaps the value of beautiful objects and scenes – and their moral significance – rests on the fact that if there *were* to be human valuers (even if there will not be), they would value them.

Trees, mountains and oceans

The moral embrace, as seen, should certainly extend to non-human experiencing creatures that have a conscious point of view; we ought not to promote unnecessary suffering. We have a grasp of what it is to act in the interests of other conscious creatures. Let us sympathize with Shel Silverstein's musing:

Oh how I once loved tuna salad,
Pork and lobsters, lamb chops too,
'Til I stopped and looked at dinner,
From the dinner's point of view.

Many take matters further, wanting not only to be vegetarian, to save the individual whale in distress and to block animal experimentation, but also to respect butterflies, palm trees and, possibly, even mosquitoes. We enter ecological 'green' ethics.

Ecological ethics may be defended in an easily understandable way. The environment and living items, including those without consciousness – insects, trees, a wilderness, a species – possess instrumental value, usefulness for humans. Individual whales may have interests, the species does not; but the species has instrumental value as does the forest and non-conscious creatures. The creatures' genetic constitutions may aid future medical research; preservation of environments is essential for so-called ecological balance, necessary for human survival. All is not, though, easy sailing in the world of the greens. Conflict can exist between animal liberationists and conservationists: to cull may be necessary in order to conserve. Conflict also exists between those who approach these matters by placing their faith in free markets and those who are troubled by the 'free market' generation of a throwaway culture, with ever-increasing human wants, leading to depletion of natural resources and a scarring of nature and creatures' habitats through non-degradable waste disposals.

Instead of instrumentalist factors, we may, though, focus on how all living beings, including trees and insects, are teleological centres. We can spot what is good for a butterfly, a tree, a plant. They have a good of their own, even though they lack awareness. Because of that good of their own, it is argued, they possess intrinsic worth. Their 'good of their own' contrasts with what we have in mind when speaking of a good wine; we do not wish for the good of our wine, notes Aristotle, but that it keeps, so that it tastes good for us. That relativity may also apply to some extent when we clip and train bushes and trees; we are satisfying our aesthetic senses rather than working on what is good for the bush, the tree.

If teleological centres are accepted as possessing intrinsic worth, a moral claim may come into play: we should respect items with intrinsic worth. True, we cannot help all ailing creatures – all collapsing storm-damaged trees – but that does not undermine their intrinsic worth and hence moral value. True, too, in many cases we prioritize human welfare over, say, that of malarial mosquitoes, mice or even chimps; but that fails to show that such beings merit no moral regard. Overall, the view calls for nature to be respected.

Going for the deepest 'green'

We may enter more deeply into the ecological green and argue that the wilderness, the desert, the oceans possess intrinsic value, and not mere instrumental value for the benefit of humans and other animals. Humans are part of the global ecology – we are within a community of organisms, of Mother Earth or Gaia – and so we ought positively to value the global and our position within. That seems, though, to possess the taint of self-interest rather than morality; we are anxious about Gaia because we are part of Gaia.

A distinctive green position with a degree of depth, 'deep green', is that environmental items, such as deserts, rainforests and the wilderness, have value independently of human purposes. We may be concerned to protect a wilderness, valuing its existence, even though – its being a wilderness – most of us will not be permitted to visit it. Matters blur a little: maybe we value the wilderness because we simply like knowing of its presence; thus our existence remains essential to its value. That liking, though, is a far cry from valuing the wilderness for its usefulness. Similarly, we typically prefer diversity to more of the same: the continuation of lions and tigers strikes us as preferable to having just lots more lions and no tigers – whether or not we often meet with them.

The deep green position just outlined assumes that the environment would lack value, were there no beings who valued it. A more radical claim – the deepest, deepest green – is that some items, the sunset, the wilderness, even a pebble, possess value completely independently of human (or any other) valuers. That presents the strongest understanding of intrinsic value. There can be planetary movements when no conscious beings exist to perceive them; and natural items can possess value, even if no valuers exist to value them. Consider a Last Man scenario, derived from Richard Routley. Maybe there has been a great disaster:

> You are the last man in the universe. You are about to die. You are facing the Okavango delta or the snow and ice terrain of Antarctic, or even simply the flat plains of the Fens. Suppose that now, just before you die, you could blow up and utterly destroy what is before you – everything. Would you be doing anything wrong?

The original scenario encouraged recognition that values extend beyond human welfare; attention was on the non-human animals remaining. Perhaps, though, the destruction could also be wrong because of some natural beauty. Perhaps it is wrong to eradicate parts of nature – for the sheer fun of it – even if that nature lacks conscious beings. Maybe it would also be wrong to destroy magnificent works of art, architecture and archaeological remains – also the originals or last remaining copies or scores of great literature and music – even though no one would ever again experience them.

The motivating thought here could simply and less mysteriously be that wanton destruction is wrong. Maybe the default position should be an attitude of care towards the world in which we find ourselves and towards the accomplishments of others. That, of course, fails to show that some natural scenes, some accomplishments, possess intrinsic value, whereas others do not. We find ourselves once again with a dilemma, akin to that of the *Euthyphro*, but here, for example, relating to beauty. Is the sunset beautiful because we have welcoming feelings towards it – or do we have such feelings because it is beautiful?

Putting the environment to one side, we typically value people; people are valuers, valuing some items, disvaluing others. Valuers would seem to possess intrinsic value. Even if we valuers did not value valuers, including ourselves, would not valuers still be valuable? 'No, they are valuable only if we value them,' is a reply, to which the retort could be, 'Well, that at least perhaps suggests that valuings, and hence valuers, are intrinsically valuable.' With one intrinsic value thus justified – if it is – maybe we can edge along to others, discovered by our paying careful attention or reflecting clearly – maybe, opening ourselves to a proper *feeling* – about these matters.

♈

We have seen how morality may spread its wings, taking us way beyond concerns for individual human lives to a regard for other animals, species, trees – for *their* sake – and even to a regard for oceans and mountains; perhaps they possess intrinsic value or at least merit awe, even piety. How far to go provokes some anxiety;

what justifies the lengths to which we should or should not go remains a puzzle.

We have also seen how worries about what merits value may return us to questions about what sort of individuals we should be and be pleased to be – surely, not the sort that engages in wanton destruction of valleys and mountains. Indeed, it is appropriate, highly appropriate, when drawing near to closing a book on ethics, to reflect further on lives that we could embrace with relish – rightly with relish.

We need to muse on the ethos of being human; we need to muse on human being.

10

'For every foot, its own shoe'

We are dying animals. We know that one day we shall be no more – well, no more on this mortal coil. Religious believers hope for life eternal, but few would be certain of that hope fulfilled. Certain or not, we may reflect upon life, upon our individual lives so fleeting: have we lived as we should? Have *I* lived as I should? I may wonder whether I have led a good life, whether I could or should have been morally more clear-sighted; perhaps I ought to have resisted morality – at least conventional morality – and lived very differently, with greater or less decorum, rebelliously even, even as an iconoclast. Morality most naturally concerns duties to others; we also have duties to ourselves, of how we should be.

We typically want to live well, yet we are creatures battered by events beyond our control, living within circumstances not of our making, finding ourselves with lusts, reflections and fears, often beyond our ken, our understanding. Sometimes whatever we do, we do wrong. The batterings, perils and seductions, vary from person to person. The way in which one person flourishes may differ radically from that of neighbours: the good life for one may be no good for another. The good life, for a few, may even be that of the silent cell, of earthly austerity, with eyes cast upward to the heavens or forwards to Heaven on Earth.

Being of the same species, we have needs in common. 'Grub first, then ethics' was Bertold Brecht's realistic instruction. With life's necessities settled – though we should rightly recoil from doing anything, just anything, for personal survival – we may try to determine how best to live. We may judge that things have gone well – until, on reflection, we realize we were blind to the good things in life. Those who grasped continually at worldly goods may later reflect how impoverished that grasp came to be. The quick response could be, 'Do not reflect' – but a life without reflection is no human life at all – and, however tightly closed our eyes, our life's undesirable features would remain.

'For every foot, its own shoe,' wrote Montaigne. We may well see how that footwear difference could carry over to individuals' flourishing. We may, though, wonder how far it carries, if far at all, regarding morality's demands. We surely cannot select a morality at will. However hard some will it otherwise, killing Jews because they are Jews, or Palestinians because they are Palestinians, is morally wrong, deeply morally wrong – full stop.

Beyond morality

In economics examinations, it is quipped, the questions each year are exactly the same; that helps candidates not at all because, each year, the *correct* answers are different. Regarding best ways of living, answers also seem to differ, from culture to culture, from generation to generation. That fails, though, to show differences in underlying moral anxieties; anxieties may remain constant and universal, yet because of surrounding differences they are manifested differently. In cultures without contraception, premarital sexual intercourse may be condemned, yet in ones with contraception, be permitted; the same moral concern is present for happiness and avoidance of unwanted children. You seek comfort when you walk outside; in winter you wear a coat, in summer no coat at all.

Differences in factual beliefs can lead to different moral practices, despite common underlying morality. Assume worry about human welfare: then, if you are sure that eternal damnation awaits women dressed immodestly, it is your moral duty to insist on modesty. If you are convinced that a fourteen-day-old foetus is en-souled and a person, then you should vehemently oppose abortion. Such cases do not support moral relativism; they should encourage reflection on the convictions, assessing whether justified. So far, we are not beyond morality.

Despite different practices, whether in ancient Athens, South America, or twenty-first-century Europe, most recognize the importance of human welfare, fairness, respecting (certain) others – and appreciation of sunset and song. That recognition, of course, does not prevent immoralities – of children in Victorian England being sent up chimneys, of US Southern states once clinging to racial segregation and of many desperate refugees today afforded no refuge at all.

'Ethics' and 'morality' have been used synonymously, but 'ethics' sometimes moves beyond the moral – to values that may even take precedence over the moral. An influential example is based on the painter Gauguin. Although historically inaccurate, it suggests challenges to both morality's supremacy and its immunity to luck.

> Gauguin, failing in business, convinced that he was an artist, a painter, deserted his wife and five children, escaped from the 'artificial and conventional' by sailing to Tahiti to paint – and, we should add, engage in dusky sexual exploits with dusky young maidens. His paintings, in due course, became much admired for their experimentation in colour; they were seen to possess considerable aesthetic merit, influencing twentieth-century art.

Here, morality – conventional morality at least – took second place to aesthetic values. The fictional Gauguin ignored his moral obligations, seeing his painterly work of greater significance.

For another example, consider again the biblical Abraham on the verge of sacrificing his son Isaac in accordance, it seemed, with God's wishes. Whether it is a tortuous tale, showing God's opposition to sacrifice – who knows? Such sacrifice, though, is deeply morally wrong. Abraham was prepared to undertake it, valuing the religious above the moral. With a country's security at risk, political leaders may approve torturing suspected terrorists, despite knowing torture's immorality. Recognizable moral duties – do not sacrifice; do not torture – are here, it seems, overridden by other values. That claim may be contested; divinity and state security readily possess moral aspects. Let us stay then with Gauguin and the aesthetic.

Kantian-inspired deontologists would insist that Gauguin acted as he ought not to have done – whatever the outcome for his life and art. Moral values override. Utilitarians could argue that Gauguin did the right thing because, as it transpired, greater overall happiness was achieved – via pleasures to art lovers – compared with the happiness, had he remained as loyal spouse, father and salesman failing to sell. That shoehorning of all values into pleasures disregards art's intrinsic value; it has regard solely for pleasures garnered. Recall: if all value is grounded in pleasure, we could skip the paintings, music and poetry – the cherry blossom, love and conversation – and just seek injections that deliver required pleasurable sensations.

In contrast to utilitarian and Kantian lines, some, perhaps inspired by Socrates, could insist that even if Gauguin sincerely believed his life overall had gone well, justifying abandonment of his family, really it had not gone well. Flourishing necessarily requires embracing the moral virtues – in this case, not letting down his family, despite painterly talent. Moral failure contaminated his flourishing, his living well.

That we may be pleased about Gauguin's commitment to art, accepting his immorality as justified, rests on the good luck of his painterly success. His venture could have gone wrong; his sailing could have ended in disaster or his work been tenth-rate. His bad behaviour towards his family would then have taken centre stage. His luck was an ethical rather than a moral luck. Had he been unsuccessful or successful, many, as said, would proclaim his actions immoral; but, according to some, any immorality here is overwhelmed by the good luck of artistic achievement. He can stand by his life, well-disposed to how it went. We may have a purchase on his values. His way of life – his ethos, his ethics – took him beyond morality. That still raises questions of whether he should affirm his earlier immorality even though it led to his life being fulfilled. Recall the Paralympics example (p. 162).

Dilemmas – being morally ensnared

How can we handle ethical dilemmas? Dilemmas often are far from the moral, the ethical, but simply the trivial of what to tick off next on the 'to do' list – no moral matter unless the ticking be by utilitarians, obsessed with calculating happiness.

Move to the moral. Both Abe and Zoe are dying; they will be upset if you fail to visit. Worse, they will be upset if you see the other. With such dilemmas, ignoring other factors, a principled answer may exist by way of distress calculation. Such a calculation, in practice, is, though, pretty mythical. In any case, whatever you do, you will do something wrong; you are morally ensnared.

Moral and ethical traps also arise when incommensurable values clash: if you tell the boss what really happened, you undermine your friendship with colleagues; if you work to become a great painter, you let down your family. Those dilemmas are profound, not mere utilitarian calculative difficulties; and they do not arise because alternative actions lead to the same quantity of hedonic outcomes, with resort to coin-spinning for solutions. They arise because ethics, including morality, attends to an eclectic collection of values.

No science, no accountancy, is available to resolve ethical dilemmas – to measure the value of family life against a career; or freedom of speech against the nation's security. No calculation took place, leading E. M. Forster to conclude, 'If I had to choose between betraying my country and betraying my friend, I hope I should have the guts to betray my country.'

There is no formal deduction, no formal induction – and no voice from the heavens to guide in such matters. Rather, dialogue, comparisons and contrasts form the reasoning. In courts of law, as John Wisdom would stress, judges hear the evidence, bring together past cases, precedents and what the law says. They then 'weigh' matters, compare cases with cases, maybe concluding that the defendants were negligent or acted unreasonably; other expert judges may judge differently. Hence, majority votes often determine legal outcomes; that should remind us of the fragility of some verdicts of guilt or innocence – whether at local court level or the Supreme Court.

Regarding individuals' dilemmas, majority votes have no foothold. Instead, we may discuss with others, with ourselves, coming to view matters anew, as in a drawing we can see a duck figure transformed into a rabbit, or landscapes as now conveying melancholy. Wisdom tells of a woman trying on a new hat, wondering if it is suitable for the occasion in mind. She is undecided. Her friend, gazing, suddenly announces, 'The Taj Mahal!' With that, the buying indecision vanishes. The hat is not right. That transformation, that knowledge, appears mysterious – but it happens. Comments can suddenly make us see differently.

Although considerations brought to bear lack formal structuring, they are not thereby to be dismissed as worthless. As the Cambridge literary critic F. R. Leavis would emphasize, in evaluations of novels – of any works of art – the dialogue is of the form, 'This is so, is it not?' met by 'Yes, but…' We draw attention to different features; they vie with each other for highest priority.

After discussion, after reflection, *the* right thing to do – you ought to do A, not B – may become clear, though often it will not. That does not mean a definitive right answer must exist, but we lack ability to find it. How can the factors on Sartre's student (pp. 110–12) even theoretically be measured against each other?

LIVES – FOR THOUGHT

Socrates: His last days in 399 BC are described in Plato's *Phaedo*. Plato tells of Socrates, having accepted the Athenian verdict condemning him to death, duly drinking the hemlock:

> Such was the end of our friend, concerning whom I may truly say, that of all the men of his time whom I have known, he was the wisest and justest and best.

Pyrrhus: This King of Epirus, making plans for conquest, is speaking to his confidant Cineas:

> 'We will first conquer the rest of Greece,' he said. 'And afterwards?' said Cineas. 'We will overtake Africa.' 'After Africa?' 'We will go on to Asia, we will conquer Asia Minor, Arabia.' 'And then?' 'We will go all the way to the Indies.' 'After the Indies?' 'Ah!' said Pyrrhus, 'I will rest.' 'Why don't you,' said Cineas, 'rest to begin with?'

A rare being: Goldsworthy Lowes Dickinson (1862–1932), Goldie, was a fellow of King's College, Cambridge, a humanist, yet no great philosopher, author or reformer. E. M. Forster wrote of him:

> He was never shipwrecked or in peril, he was seldom in great bodily pain, never starved or penniless, he never confronted an angry mob nor was sent to prison for his opinions… From a material point of view, Fate gave him an easy time, which he frankly appreciated.

He was, though – and could one want for anything more? –

> beloved, affectionate, unselfish, intelligent, witty, charming – qualities fused into such an unusual creature… He did not merely increase our experience: he left us more alert for what has not yet been experienced and more hopeful about other men because he had lived.

José Matada: In 2012 in Angola, he stowed in a plane's undercarriage. Hours later, he fell from the sky, landing in a London street – dead. Brought up during Mozambique's wars, suffering hardships unknown to us, yet kind and gentle, he sought a better life. Millions are as desperate, even more so, than Matada, though not so foolish. Can we live well only by closing eyes to such misery – and if we do close eyes, are *we* living well?

How much ought caring for a mother to count compared with avenging a brother? Security of the state justifies detention without charge for how long? Is it for three days, three months or ten years? Does loyalty to a friend have greater value than loyalty to your country? If it does, to what extent? Decisions have to be made even though 'we cannot decide'. So we decide – and what we do will be something wrong (say, abandoning the mother) and also something right (say, fighting in the Resistance). Later, we may admire the decision – or live with regret.

Iris Murdoch tells of a mother-in-law (M) and the daughter (D) married to her son. M behaves beautifully throughout the daughter's stay with her, yet, from the start, M has a low opinion of D. Let us add: M made the decision to put up with D staying, though she could have said 'no'. Murdoch's tale continues:

> M finds D quite a good-hearted girl, but while not exactly common
> yet certainly unpolished and lacking in dignity and refinement.
> D is inclined to be pert and familiar, insufficiently ceremonious,
> brusque, sometimes positively rude, always tiresomely juvenile.

Later, M discovers the daughter 'to be not vulgar but refreshingly simple, not undignified but spontaneous, not noisy but gay, not tiresomely juvenile but delightfully youthful'. M has been engaged in active vision, paying closer attention to the daughter. She sees the daughter in a new light. Her decision to let the daughter stay has turned out right.

We can be helped to see – to deal with dilemmas – through the arts, through imaginative constructions of people's lives, be they staged, on paper or in music. Some find help through faith. 'I believe in Christianity as I believe that the sun has risen: not only because I see it, but because by it I see everything else,' declared C. S. Lewis. Religious glasses are sometimes worn for the better; sometimes considerably for the worse. Witness Shia/Sunni conflicts within Islam; witness earlier crusades in the name of Christ.

Through the arts, be they plays, novels, operas or even television soap-operas, our emotions and perceptivity can be enriched; we may grasp people's behaviour as far more nuanced than simply right or wrong, good or bad. We learn how people are churlish, spiteful or bumptious – couth, dignified, struggling to stand up for principles – serious, puckish or witty. We see the world normatively in shades of colour; we see behaviour from different perspectives of human consciousness. Scientific understandings are of no help with such shadings and perspectives; poetry, as John Stuart Mill found, can be of considerable help.

Music with words, by way of opera, sometimes offers sublime experiences in which our self-interest is lost – the self is lost – yet, back with oneself, those fictional worlds may play in the imagination and aid our grasp of everyday struggles, hopes and sorrows. Indeed, pure music – symphonies, sonatas, string quartets – music that cannot be put into words, may yet uplift and widen eyes on the world, on the ethos of living and upon how to be. That endorsement is no elitism, but a gesture against the mistaken portrayal of classical music and especially opera – and other cultures' high art – as now out of bounds save for a select few. What may improve the ethos of a life, as Mill would argue, should be available to all. Excellence – be it at cooking, piano-playing or chess – rarely comes without a struggle; and time, careful listening and a generosity in spirit are needed to give 'difficult' music a chance to weave its influence and mysterious uplift. 'All things excellent,' wrote Spinoza, 'are as difficult as they are rare.' Well, we may aim to reduce that rarity.

That music uplifts, let it hastily be added, should not encourage the dewy-eyed. Although tempted to assert music's civilizing power, we should remember those Nazis, appreciative of Mozart and Beethoven, who, incongruously, would force starving Jewish musicians, concentration camp inmates, to play the great works, those tributes to humanity. So committed were the cultured Nazis to their ideology, they could see no value in music composed with Jewish taints, such as the music of Mendelssohn and Schoenberg.

They are both right

Two people in the same situation, agreed on the facts, engaging in the same moral musings and wider ethical reflections, reach opposing decisions, taking different paths. Is one right, the other wrong? In factual matters, if two people hold contradictory beliefs, then indeed one is right, the other wrong. If two people disagree over which horse will win the race, they cannot both be right. In matters of value, things are different.

Suppose two women, medical students, are in the same position regarding whether, ethically, they ought to go ahead with an abortion. Having a child will disrupt their studies, their plans to make their mark in the medical world; also, it looks as if the child will be born handicapped. They know that the decision is not to be treated frivolously. They have the same emotional pulls, anxieties and moral worries. If the right decision is to have the abortion for Andrea, then surely it should be the right decision for Bethany. To quote Sidgwick committed to morality's universality:

> We cannot judge an action to be right for A and wrong for B, unless we can find in the natures or circumstances of the two some difference which we can regard as a reasonable ground for difference in their duties. If therefore I judge any action to be right for myself, I judge it to be right for any other person whose nature and circumstances do not differ from my own in important respects.

In opposition, we recommend sympathy for the following thought: Andrea concludes that going ahead with the abortion is the right thing to do; Bethany concludes that continuing with the pregnancy is the right thing. There need be no contradiction. It is possible that they could both be right in their decisions. Of course, they could both be wrong – or one right, one wrong.

The two women have ended up differently. Many may insist, as Sidgwickians, that therefore a relevant difference must have existed in their values or circumstances. That insistence is ungrounded. Perhaps the sole ethically relevant difference is that they decide to act differently: one goes ahead; the other does not. The difference arises only because of what they do. We may say, flimsily, that they are making themselves different; that makes the difference.

The above is no recommendation for relativism or subjectivism. Andrea's belief that abortion is the right path for her does not guarantee that it is right. Thinking something right, even after considerable reflection, does not usually make it right. That is readily shown.

First, people may have made decisions – be they concerning abortion, euthanasia, whistle-blowing – but not treated matters seriously enough; that very fact could paint their characters in unethical colours. Some matters matter; they are too important to solve by spinning coins. Secondly, people, seriously minded, earnest, may simply have seen things wrongly; recall Murdoch's mother-in-law.

Returning to Andrea and Bethany, it may later become clear how they should assess their earlier decisions. An action being right need not depend solely on what led to the decision; it may rest on how things develop. The way things turn out could show the women that their different decisions were both right – or could leave them both uncertain or changing their assessments as the years pass. Those possibilities are inherent in many ethical dilemmas. Both Andrea and Bethany sought to do what was best. We may see them as both being drawn by the Good, though it is unlikely that they expressed matters that way.

Wittgenstein heard of a man who had decided that he must either leave his wife or abandon his cancer research. Wittgenstein's reported response was:

Suppose I am his friend and I say to him, 'Look, you've taken this girl out of her home, and now, by God, you've got to stick to her.' This would be called taking up an ethical attitude. He may reply, 'But what of suffering humanity? How can I abandon my research?' In saying this he may be making it easy for himself: he wants to carry on that work anyway… And he may be inclined to view the effect on his wife relatively easily: 'It probably won't be fatal for her. She'll get over it, probably marry again' – And so on.

Wittgenstein goes on to note that it may not be that way at all.

It may be that he has a deep love for her. And yet he may think that if he were to give up his work he would be no husband for her… Here we may say that we have all the materials of a tragedy; and we could only say: 'Well, God help you.' Whatever he finally does, the way things then turn out may affect his attitude. He may say, 'Well, thank God I left her; it was better all around.' Or maybe, 'Thank God I stuck to her.'… Or it may be just the opposite.

Empathy is appropriate here. People can find themselves in tragic 'impossible situations', sometimes of their own making; sometimes not. They have to do something – and what they do, they may later regret, feeling forever remorse, or later stand by, even proud. What, at a particular time, is viewed as an unfortunate path, in retrospect can have success writ large.

Baffling behaviour by characters in a play can become comprehensible by curtain fall. An apparently lousy formation for 'white' in chess becomes inspired, if leading to a win – though luck probably played a part. Developments in architecture and literature may only be properly understood once later artistic movements arise; as Jorge Luis Borges noted, 'Every writer creates his own precursors.' Similarly, whether an action was ethically right, or wrong, can rest on how life evolves and is shaped – though it may not. Perhaps Gauguin's desertion is forever a blot.

Lamentations: what if the whole of my life has been wrong?

Although deep puzzles exist concerning the nature of the 'self', we must grasp ourselves as continuing, as acting with a past and future, with things going well – or badly – as life unfolds. Kierkegaard summed this up in his 1843 *Journal*:

> It is perfectly true, as the philosophers say, that life must be understood backwards. But they forget the other proposition, that it must be lived forwards.

We are not inkwells, inert; we are not rivers that flow with no choice of direction. While alive, there exists the possibility of seeing or casting matters in new perspectives, acting afresh; our lives become understood differently, taking on different hues. We can re-form ourselves. As Kierkegaard wrote:

> It becomes more and more evident that life can never really be understood in time simply because at no particular moment can I find the necessary resting place from which to understand it – backwards.

'It ain't over till the fat lady sings' – well, so it is said. There is no resting place until death. To understand a life, we need sight of its contours, its development, of how past events influenced the later. We cannot grasp the nature of a chess game or even just of checkmate solely from seeing an end position of a checkmate; and a snapshot of a life, by the end, does not tell us how that life was.

A life overall is no sum of its parts independently assessed. Even if we judged a life solely by net pleasures, there would remain significant differences between a life that commenced high with pleasure but continually declined – and one with an opposite profile. Aware of life's rises and falls, we may feel for the ancient

Greek Mimnermos's lamentation at losing golden Aphrodite. 'Let me die when these things mean nothing to me, secretive lovemaking and sweet gifts and the bed.' In old age, evil cares wear down the mind; God, says Mimnermos, has made old age a burden. The ethical regard for how to live must hence include regard for how to die.

When painful dying comes into view, some override any moral commitment to life being sacred, a gift from God, not to be taken; they may seek the courage to die with dignity, at the proper time for them – and they may seek help to do so. Others rage against death – 'against the dying of the light' – with courage and determination to remain alive as long as possible. Yet others, to quote Samuel Beckett, 'have neither the courage to end it, nor the strength to go on'.

A life immortal, though, even un-ageing, everlasting here on Earth or in a celestial elsewhere – or be it eternal, nowhere and no-when – runs the risk of no coherent structure. It would scarcely be human living, if untroubled by dangers and the deaths of others – and if without awareness of eventual finality. No urgency would arise for the morrow, no fear of global warming, no need for physical courage. Were the immortality disembodied, numerous anxieties would be absent, as would be delights of feasting, ravishing smiles and seashore walks. With no end to our time, getting things done would have, it seems, reduced value. Arguably, we need mortality for life to have value, for life to have shape.

Although personal mortality appears essential to the ethos of a human life, perhaps we still need others to carry forward the human flame – after we have gone. Consider the P. D. James tale in which all humans become infertile: what values could then give meaning to life, when *all* humanity would soon be lost? Would research into cancer prevention, planning great architectural wonders, composing symphonies, planting trees, still be worthwhile? Do we need others to exist – 'collective after-living' – for our own mortal life, lacking any afterlife, to make sense?

A sting in death, with others surviving, is that we become, in Sartre's bleak words, 'prey to the living', to the Other. Once deceased, we are impotent; others can sum up our lives, fix, classify and judge us. 'It ain't over even when the fat lady sits down.'

'What a pity that he didn't make more of his life.' 'She ought to have risked leaving her job and concentrated on her trumpet-playing.' 'Looking back, they were such bores and so pretentious.' Despite being Sartre's prey, post-death events can be of benefit. Given her particular interests, publication of her life's work, although posthumous, is good; his loved garden continuing to be tended and cherished shows our respect for him. Our selves extend beyond our living skin to our interests, projects and reputation (recall betrayal, p. 67); those interests *et al.* – and hence we – can be harmed or benefited even when we are no more.

Deaths of public figures these days are announced with, we may feel, unseemly haste: urgent newsflashes, commentators vying to be first to sum up the departed, often with exaggerated, obsequious praise almost as indecent as later attacks on reputations. Further, the privilege of 'public innocence until found guilty in law' evaporates, it seems, once deceased. Whatever wrongs in the lives of those now dead, there should still be space – ethical space – for some respect. There are good and bad ways of treating the dead.

A tragedy is not just that life may end too soon – or linger for too long – but that life can offer too much. 'You can't always get what you want', pranced the Rolling Stones. The reasons differ. The good life of a faithful family man cannot exist with his engaging the good life as Casanova. That is a matter of logic. Saving the whale may upset a life devoted to research into medieval philosophy. That is a matter of time. And Gauguin's quest for artistic success blotted his marriage – perhaps a matter of personality.

Tolstoy's character Ivan Ilyich highlights an anxiety of mortality that we can and perhaps should confront. Nearing the end of life, worse than his physical sufferings were his mental sufferings:

LOSING THE SELF

Metaphysics into Ethics: We think of ourselves persisting into the future: we make plans for holidays and retirements; yet what constitutes being the same person months, or years, even just days, ahead?

Difficulties in answering can suggest that the persisting self is illusory. Your concern for your future 'self' is for someone bearing various psychological similarities with your 'self' now. Your concern for your future is, in a sense, concern for someone else. That metaphysical thought leads to the proposal that concern for others now is as rational as for your 'future self'. Perhaps there is no great divide between self-interest and other-interest.

Loss of privacy – a malign loss: Invasions of privacy were once easily understood: people peered through keyholes or steamed letters open. Invasions now are ever invasive, via CCTV, tracking phone use and online searches. Soon, glasses, even tattoos, will reveal our locations, exposing us to buying pressures as we near stores eager for business. Still, our private thoughts remain distinct and safe – but wait... Why not play the ideas, temptations, desires, straight into our neurology – why stop at the skin? One day, shall we be at a loss over which thoughts and feelings are 'our own' – even over the very idea of a private life of 'our own'?

Losing oneself – a benign loss: Activities are often just means to ends; we want to further a project, reduce our weight or give ourselves pleasure. In contrast, we can lose ourselves in games of chess, in playing tennis, where the value can be the good game played, set by its rules, not by external glows of winning or prizes received.

We can lose ourselves in conversation, in glancing at loved ones – in paintings, plays, novels – and especially in music, be it jazz, string quartets or opera. Losing oneself has no end in view. Returning to the world, we may, though, be emotionally enhanced, more perceptive of others. Curiously, we may be unable to put that into words; it may show in our sensitivity. Can we express in words what, say, Beethoven's late string quartets mean?

'What if in reality my whole life has been wrong?' It occurred to him that what had appeared utterly impossible the night before – that he had not lived his life as he should have done – might after all be true.

Ilyich tried to defend his life, his reluctance to fight authority, yet his case was weak; Ilyich was leaving this life, aware that there was no putting it right. 'What then?' asked Ilyich.

Some people may feel for Ilyich's plight; they worry whether they have obeyed God or obeyed the right god. For many, though, the Ilyichian question presupposes a detachment one giant leap too far: how could we assess a life, without using the values in our possession? In reply, here is at least a stab at some detachment.

We grant that things have not gone well for a young woman who, because of an accident, suffers severe brain damage. She is now perfectly content, unaware of her mental impairment, of her loss of bright future. She gets everything that she now values – warmth, food and repeated child cartoons playing – yet things have not gone well for her. Were she to detach herself from her condition, she would agree that things have gone badly.

A man once caring, kindly, with affection for others, because of a brain tumour and surgery becomes cold, indifferent, self-centred. If he could step outside and see the change, he would be appalled at the ethos of his new life; he would see it as tragic.

Reflect on the contented lives of some non-human animals. In cold Cambridge winters, the philosopher John McTaggart Ellis McTaggart would allow his cat Pushkin to sit close by the fire, while he, McTaggart, shivered at his desk, philosophizing. Why give the best place to the cat? Well, he would reply, warmth by a blazing fire is the best that it gets for a cat. We judge that a human life has more going for it than a feline's.

Some people feel queasy about judging other people's lives and values; yet we frequently do such judging, and often we ought.

Judgment need be no elitist imposition of values, but acceptance that some things in life are good, some things bad – and encouragement for others to open eyes and see. We should, of course, also step back from our own life; we ought not to wait for an Ilychian deathbed scene. 'Is the whole of my life wrong so far?'

'Would you not curse the demon?'

Pretend that you must live your life again and again, without any difference whatever. Are you so proud of your life and its ways so far, asked Nietzsche, that you could embrace an eternal recurrence?

Eternal recurrence is nonsensical; if your repeated lives are exactly the same, they collapse into one life – this very one. Despite the nonsense, the eternal recurrence, this imaginative thought experiment, urges us to accept responsibility for what we do, for how we live, for how we die. As Nietzsche wrote: if told of such an eternal recurrence,

> would you not throw yourself down and gnash your teeth and curse the demon who spoke thus?… Or how well disposed would you have to become to yourself and to life – to long for nothing more fervently than this ultimate eternal confirmation and seal?

'How should *I* fill my life?' One person's filling may differ from another's: recall Andrea and Bethany. Morality demands a voice in any life; but life needs more – and less. Life completely engulfed in performing moral duties – dogged devotion to supporting the weak, always detached, always fair – would lack substance for most, and likely for us all, if those supported also lived solely for duty. To live only for others if those others also live only for others lacks ultimate substance. It is akin to the vacuity of commanding someone to follow this command when the command is nothing more than 'Follow this command'.

Human living – to be human – involves attachments, accomplishments, diversities. We need time for our 'selves', our relationships, *our* projects, be they flute-playing, bird-watching or family life – be they talking the sun down with friends, smiling through repartee or participating in games and play. We have some options over dances and dance partners, but biology and common humanity ensure that, ethically, some we cannot refuse.

Typically, we value some arts: magnificent cathedrals, miniature gardens and being enraptured by song. We admire the Parthenon; we quietly forget the broken backs upon which it, and cathedrals and mosques, were built. We are probably pleased that certain artists closed eyes to the moral, producing arresting opera or finely crafted literature. We may admire cosmological explorations, defend nuclear defence upgrades and welcome prestigious City developments to the glory of developers; yet the vast sums allocated could have alleviated the anguished helplessness of millions.

Be the focus at the individual level or that of the community, there are, on the one hand, attachments to 'those close to us' and, on the other, awareness of those outside, those outside who have nothing, or virtually nothing, save despair. The ethical life, the eclectic ethical, with its mishmash of values, cannot ignore either; but how much devotion to one, when at the expense of the other? How much should *we* – our community, our country – spend helping others; how much to keep for ourselves? No formula exists to answer that question. Rest assured, though, we all know the direction of bias. The ethical life must surely make some correction for that.

♈

'All things conspire,' wrote Hippocrates – all things are interconnected. In today's world, that is easy to see, through rainforest destruction, gulf streams and butterfly wings that affect climates continents away. Indeed, interconnections are glaringly on view as these words are written, with poor African countries ravaged by the ebola virus: the US and Europe are now alert to dangers of widespread transmission; their decades of neglect of poor countries' medical facilities, of letting 'free trade' rip to the West's advantage, may after all not have been self-interestedly wise, let alone morally so.

Global communications ensure our easy awareness of tragedy: natural catastrophes, conflicts in war-torn lands, the destitute in poor countries scarcely scraping livings in producing cheap commodities for wealthy consumers elsewhere. Even were we not to be adversely affected, could we be well disposed to our lives, if blotting out that awareness?

Nietzsche, as earlier noted, asked: how can we affirm life, say 'yes' to life, when the 'yes' amounts to affirmation of worldly woes, woes interconnected with our own well-being? That is a deeper worry than we care to face. We benefit from the sufferings – present and historic – of others. Ought we not seriously to regret those sufferings, despite welcoming the benefits? At the very least, we should feel a moral ambivalence. Indeed, even if we do not benefit – 'the sufferings have nothing to do with us, no business of ours' – can we morally just stand aside and isolate ourselves? Should we not possess some human solidarity and act accordingly? It is surely a deceit to live a life – to be well disposed to that life – if in denial of a common humanity. My country, wrote Thomas Paine, is the world.

That we cannot do everything is no justification for doing nothing at all. Doing something is at least something – though it may too readily assuage our unease. We have justified concerns for ourselves and justified concerns for others; we muddle through.

Epilogue:
'Buddy, can you spare a dime?'

'How ought *I* to live?' In answer, ethics opens up beyond morality, beyond moral duty, to aesthetics, religion, sensitivities, courtesies – and to muddles and mysteries. Our eyes therefore also need to open; they need to open to small matters of living, as well as to the large.

We should rightly have low opinions of those who snarl their way through life, crashing into passers-by without apology – or with dirty shoes on train seats – oblivious to the needs of others. We may yet feel compassion for them in their blindness, so closed are they to fellow-feeling. To whom do we, *should* we, warm? The young man who deliberately scares neighbours with his dogs, nurtured into savagery? Or the young man when not at home, who leaves classical music playing for pet guinea pigs? Whether the pigs of guinea possess classical appreciation – or musical ears at all – such sensitivity, creature-feeling, such awareness of the mystery of different lives, of radically different perspectives on the world, is, without doubt, valuable, belonging to an ethical ethos.

Can we truly value ourselves, if we turn away a buddy – an old friend, who has struck hard times – asking us to spare a dime? We surely cannot be proud of a life devoted solely to self-interested pleasures. If pleasure is all that matters, then, as Nietzsche quipped, the best life is to be tickled to death. Do people truly flourish if their lifelong passion is asset accumulation and tax avoidance – anything to escape solidarity with community welfare? Perhaps they need to recall King Midas's plight. True, they may shrug their shoulders, insisting they live well – and that's an end of the matter. That is, though, no end of the matter. With reflection, most should see that there is more to what counts than what can be counted.

Whether religious or atheist, optimist or pessimist, welcoming our biological life or not, many of us easily recognize the sense of Jesus' words:

> For what shall it profit a man, if he shall gaine the whole world,
> and lose his owne soule?

There is no need to believe in the soul to warm to that sentiment, no requirement to believe in Judgement Day to grasp what is meant and sense its importance.

To live well is to acknowledge, even to embrace, our frailties, failures and foibles – and the mishmash of values in which we swim, often with the danger of drowning. To live well is yet to live with eyes uplifted, aspiring to what can be recognized as good, be it found shimmering in metaphorical heavens, in the Christian Eternity, or in soaring voices of choral music – be it found in the kaleidoscopic colours of the natural world, musings with friends, gambollings of humour, or observing the lives of pigeons.

The ethical life has many guises, yet underlying are some basic concerns, some pressing anxieties. With whom should we dance – and in which dance? We cannot sit through some dances of life; whatever we do – and fail to do – is an engagement with the lives of others, sometimes for better, sometimes for worse.

To live well is also to spread the word – to share what can be uplifting. For simple manifestations of aspiration, of eyes uplifted, whether believer or atheist, let us be lost, undisturbed for a while, in music that transcends the surrounding world. Few, once they attend, with or without hope in another, can be blind to the inspiring beauty of Thomas Tallis's *Spem in Alium*.

Coming down to earth, we rightly challenge others over their greed, their delight in power and status – and still others over their cowardice, their waste of a life and lives of yet others. We should also challenge ourselves – even more so. It is wise to remember regarding others and regarding ourselves:

Before you judge a man, you must walk a mile in his shoes.

Understanding behaviour can lead to seeing characters in new lights, from different perspectives, perhaps with empathy, however disreputable they are on first appearances. We may grasp how they have been rocked by events not of their making.

Understanding, urged Spinoza, is key to the good life, to blessedness. In understanding, in explaining others as summations of causes, we may, though, end up treating them as no different from physical barriers to surmount; and barriers merit no sympathy, no empathy. Understanding, to speak paradoxically, is no guarantee of understanding.

Yet, I am certainly so very different from being an object that I ought not to be treated as if a mere object that gets in the way.

Reflecting thus, we should then see that we cannot in fact be so different from others; there exists a common humanity meriting fellow-feeling, sparkle, even sorrow – a humanity in want of cultivation, a humanity perhaps best appreciated when acting on Forster's 'Only connect'. That is far from implying resignation, that we should, with stoical calm, submit ourselves to whatever wrongs have been done. There are times to rage.

There are also times to appreciate tragedy. Recall the driver who killed a child – no fault of his own. He would love not to be that person, not to be a killer, even accidentally so – yet tragically he is. He needs the strength to live with it, to live on. It would be inhuman to shrug it off as just one of those things. Many lives are hit by misfortunes. Others have good fortunes, not least those of missing such tragedies. Humility is needed to recognize that good fortune. Sadly, humility is often lacking.

♈

At the heart of Ethics is the feeling that we can and should do better. Ethics encourages us to stretch – to stretch our eyes, our imagination – to enhance lives and living. It provides an aspiration, of being at one with our way, or ways, of life, taking responsibility for what we have done and what we hope to do better.

Ethical reflections cannot provide a formula to save us from doing wrong or mistreating ourselves. Ethical reflections cannot shield us from surrounding sufferings and the melancholy of mortality. Their aim is not to blot out awareness of our shames, regrets and remorse over past doings. The reflections may, though, enable us to see our lives – and lives of others – in new and different colours, providing guidance for a well-disposed future.

The eclecticism of the ethics presented here, it is hoped, heightens awareness of incommensurable values with which we struggle and juggle – through which we muddle. Indeed, the backdrop to our reflections and actions should be sheer astonishment at our – so extremely unlikely, so highly improbable – existence. We are too familiar with being; we forget just how mysterious it is to be – and to be with others who also 'be'.

Ethics should enhance sensitivities to the significance of ethics, to leading a life whose ethos causes us no shame – or at least, not too much shame – a life to which eventually we may be well disposed. It is an awareness, to quote Camus, that a man without ethics is a wild beast loosed upon this world. We should add:

A man without ethics is a wild beast loosed upon himself.

Notes
and further reading

Where references and quotations are readily available through online search engines or printed editions, these notes are uncluttered with details. For reason of space, quotations in the chapters are often abbreviated, but, I hope, provide an accurate sense of the thinking.

Prologue: the moral medley

For key readings, with valuable commentary, see Fricker and Guttenplan, eds, *Reading Ethics* (2009); for short extracts, Peter Singer, ed., *Ethics* (1994). Bernard Williams, *Morality: An Introduction to Ethics* (1972) is a good beginning; for distinctive and advanced, try his *Ethics and the Limits of Philosophy* (1985) and David Wiggins, *Ethics, Twelve Lectures on the Philosophy of Morality* (2006).

Thought-provoking works, not ploughing through theories, are Williams (again), *Shame and Necessity* (1993), Raimond Gaita, *Good and Evil: An Absolute Conception* (1991), and Timothy Chappell, *Knowing what to do: Imagination, Virtue and Platonism in Ethics* (2014).

For lovers of screen reading, there is the reliable online *Stanford Encyclopaedia of Philosophy*. YouTube is a sometime good source for philosophy lectures, as are major university websites for lecture notes and readings. Very accessible is the website of the Royal Institute of Philosophy, London, its lectures and articles.

Exposure of business placing profits over well-being occurs in Jacques Peretti's programmes *The Men Who Made Us Spend* (BBC, 2014). The postcard tale is sometimes told as cards to bishops; even Noel Coward as sender has been disputed.

Chapter One: How ought we to live?

For terms, see Simon Blackburn, *The Oxford Dictionary of Philosophy*, 2nd edn (2008). Socrates appears in Plato's dialogues as gadfly, questioning, challenging: see *Apology* and dialogues in Plato, *The Last Days of Socrates*. Extracts from Hobbes, Butler, Smith and Bentham are in D. D. Raphael, ed., *British Moralists, 1650–1800* (1991). For detailed erudition on ancient Greeks' ethics, try Martha Nussbaum, *The Therapy of Desire* (1994). For emphasis on falsifiability of empirical theories, Karl Popper is your man. Particularism is well represented in Jonathan Dancy, *Ethics Without Principles* (2004). For objective normative reasons, see T. M. Scanlon, *Being Realistic about Reasons* (2014).

It has been a commonplace to define man as a rational animal; for challenge, see Jonathan Swift's *Gulliver's Travels* where the horses, the Houyhnhnms, live by reason, friendship and benevolence, manifesting decency and civility, in contrast to the uncouth physicality of the human-like Yahoos. Some have proposed man as the vain animal; others as the creature that can laugh.

Chapter Two: Utilitarianism: maximizing happiness

Recommended is Mill's *Utilitarianism* (1861/93), Roger Crisp's edition (1998). Mill on the dwarfing of men is in his highly influential *On Liberty* (1859). Jeremy Bentham's extracts and Francis Hutcheson's, in Raphael's collection above, and Henry Sidgwick, *Methods of Ethics*, 7th edn (1907), are harder going. Peter Singer, *Practical Ethics* 3rd edn (2011), offers utilitarian approaches to equality, animals, the rich and poor.

'Jim and the Indians' appears in Smart and Williams, *Utilitarianism: For and Against* (1973). Peter Geach (his death occurred during my writing this book) gave a precursor of the Jim and Tram puzzles. Ten people are trapped in a cave, water rising: all will drown unless they escape. A bulky man, trying to escape, is stuck in the sole exit, blocking their way. The only solution is to blow him up (you happen to have explosives), enabling escape for others. Geach, a traditional Catholic, opposed using the man as means to life-saving ends. A variant: the man is stuck, face down in the cave; he will be drowned in any case – unless blown up.

Lover-ism derives from family-ism's bondings: see Hursthouse, *Ethics, Humans and Other Animals* (2000). For moral paradoxes: Peter Cave, *This Sentence Is False: an introduction to philosophical paradoxes* (2009). I thank Mike Shaw for the Julian Barnes' observation. Mill's 'ceasing to charm' is from his autobiography.

Chapter Three: Deontology: 'I must not tell a lie'

Kant's works, not easy, are *Groundwork of the Metaphysics of Morals* (1785) and *The Metaphysics of Morals* (1797). See the Cambridge 2012 edition of *Groundwork,* introduced by Christine Korsgaard. Extracts from Kant and contemporary discussions are in Stephen Darwall, *Deontology* (2002). Onora O'Neill's *Acting on Principle* (2nd edn, 2013) takes us into reflective sympathetic detail. For Kant's jokes – be prepared to be underwhelmed – see his *Critique of Judgement* (1790). Kant the great Enlightenment thinker is seen not to be that enlightened, once his views on, for example, sexuality are encountered: Kant argues that masturbation is a greater moral wrong than suicide for one gains pleasure from the wrong of the former.

Focus on *prima facie* duties is found in W. D. Ross, an Oxford philosopher, Aristotelian scholar, of the early twentieth century. Curiously, Ross maintained that virtue outweighs any pleasure, however great: see his *The Right and The Good* (1930). Apparently a major conference was held on the philosophical implications of

Relativity Theory. Ross was later asked why he was absent. 'Just hoping it will all blow over', was his alleged reply.

Would Kant permit killing an innocent man? You are at the bottom of a well. An innocent man is hurled down, about to have a soft landing on you. He will live; you will be killed. You have a ray gun that you could use to disintegrate him. He is no aggressor, but are you within your rights to save yourself? Yes, another bizarre thought experiment – this time from Robert Nozick.

A non-Kantian and non-liar, the philosopher G. E. Moore was ensnared by his modesty. Bertrand Russell asked him, 'Moore, do you always speak the truth?' Moore's response was 'No', saying in effect, 'I do not always speak the truth.' Assuming Moore until then had always spoken the truth (unlikely, it is true, if only because he was fallible), what he said may seem false, but then, if so, it is true; but if true, then false – thus, the Paradox of the Liar (see my *This Sentence Is False*).

Chapter Four: Virtue ethics: a flourishing life

Aristotle's *Nicomachean Ethics* arrives in many editions. For extracts and papers: Stephen Darwall, *Virtue Ethics* (2003). A contemporary line is Rosalind Hursthouse, *On Virtue Ethics*, new edn (2001). I owe much to Rosalind on this topic through our Open University teaching. For a good man and harm: Peter Winch, *Ethics and Action* (1972). Terence Irwin, *Plato's Ethics* (1995), offers rich material on Socrates, Plato and Aristotle.

For cultural reflections, see Stefan Collini's works, and for universities and business, his *What Are Universities For?* (2012). For culture affecting 'truth', regarding suffering, try Joanna Bourke's *The Story of Pain: From Prayer to Painkillers* (2014). We may also wonder whether psychologically we can develop character traits that manifest what is morally required across a vast range of different circumstances; quite what makes a character trait so robust that it operates appropriately the same across very different situations?

The painter's night off derives from Richard Wollheim's *The Thread of Life* (1984), and Jonathan Katz helped with swallow (singular) and Greek Spring. Machiavelli's *The Prince* has influenced politicians, ruthless business leaders and salespeople. Machiavelli shows the sexism of his times: when talking of Fortuna as a woman, he adds, that to control her, it is necessary to beat and coerce her.

Chapter Five: God: dead or alive?

Much written about God is obscure, certainly to non-believers – though thanks to Timothy Vince, Howard Conder and Arthur Roderick for trying to open my eyes to biblical truth. A few believers apparently worry whether Christian missionary work should extend to any rational beings in other galaxies. For the cool, see Christopher Lewis and Dan Cohn-Sherbok, eds, *Sensible Religion* (2014), which offers sense and humanity in its readings of the great religions' holy texts – even in Jihadism properly understood. While writing this book, the not so cool was manifested by the new Islamic State in northern Iraq and Syria (ISIS), demanding that their Christians and Yazidis 'convert' to Islam or be killed: behaviour could convert; but belief?

Naturalist *non-divine* lines sometimes identify the good with what human beings, by nature, 'truly' desire or a 'perfection' being approached; but what constitutes such true desires or perfection neared? Try David Oderberg and Timothy Chappell, eds, *Human Values: New Essays on Ethics and Natural Law* (2004). Naturalist *divine* lines should be vexed by God's mysterious moves. For the Good as creatively responsible for the universe, see John Leslie's intriguing *Infinite Minds* (2001). For accessible details on the American Declaration: Danielle Allen, *Our Declaration* (2014). The Chateaubriand quotation is from David Wiggins, 'Solidarity and the Root of the Ethical' (2008); it promotes solidarity in splendid detail, linking with Simone Weil.

Classic scepticisms are: David Hume, *Dialogues Concerning Natural Religion* (1779); J. S. Mill, *Three Essays on Religion* (1850–70). Spinoza's excommunication is in Steven Nadler, *Spinoza's Heresy* (2004), his toleration and biblical criticism in Nadler's *A Book Forged in Hell* (2011). For humanist papers, see Grayling and Copson, eds, *The Wiley Blackwell Handbook of Humanism* (2015). For religion and suffering, see Peter Flood, ed., *New Problems in Medical Ethics* (1953) and Joanna Bourke mentioned above, reviewed by Gavin Francis, 'How many speed bumps?' (*LRB*, 21.08.2014). John Wisdom's gardener is in his 'Gods' in *Philosophy and Psychoanalysis* (1953).

Euthyphro is in, for example, Plato, *The Last Days of Socrates*. Benjamin Franklin wrote of how he originally saw virtue as a means to Heaven – and how he aimed, but failed, at perfection. See his *The Art of Virtue* (conceived 1732).

For this chapter's quotations: Simone Weil, *Waiting for God* (1951); Nietzsche, *Beyond Good and Evil* (1886). See also Michael Tanner's short introduction *Nietzsche* (1994). 'Übermensch', untranslated, avoids the silliness of 'superman'. For God in nature, try Roger Scruton, *The Soul of the World* (2014). Wittgenstein's degeneration comment is in Rush Rhees, ed., *Ludwig Wittgenstein: Personal Recollections* (1981). My *Humanism: A Beginner's Guide* (2009) introduces critical assessment of God, religion and evil.

Chapter Six: Existentialism: freedom and responsibility

Sartre's novel *Nausea* presents classic angst; the simplified philosophy is in his *Existentialism and Humanism* (1948), though partly repudiated; the major is *Being and Nothingness* (1943; Hazel Barnes, trans. 1957), no light read. For papers, including references to de Beauvoir, see Steven Crowell, ed., *Cambridge Companion to Existentialism* (2012); also Peter Winch, *Simone Weil: The Just Balance* (1989) and Raimond Gaita, *Good and Evil* (1991).

Gary Watson, ed., *Free Will* (2003) contains Strawson's reactive attitudes, intriguing thought experiments by Frankfurt and much more. Krupke appeared in *West Side Story* – without the judge's response. *Moral Luck*, ed. Daniel Statman (1993), includes Williams and Nagel who set the topic going. A Jewish luck-orientated question is, 'How do you make God laugh?' The answer: 'Tell him your plans'.

Chapter Seven: Morality: just an illusion?

The Dawkins is from his *The Selfish Gene* (1976/2006), p.3. A philosopher's challenge to current scientific assumptions is Thomas Nagel, *Mind and Cosmos: Why the Materialist Neo-Darwinian Conception of Nature Is Almost Certainly False* (2012).

Moore's classic is *Principia Ethica* (1903). For detail and erudition, try Alexander Miller, *An Introduction to Contemporary Metaethics* (2003). Error theory was highlighted by J. L. Mackie, *Ethics, Inventing Right and Wrong* (1977). The Russell precursor is his 'Is there an absolute good?' (1922); his emotivism is in his *Religion and Science* (1935).

A little-known anti-scepticism, with considerable sense, using Sartre, Moore and John Wisdom is Renford Bambrough, *Moral Scepticism and Moral Knowledge* (1979). My thinking has mingled with Wisdom's and Bambrough's approaches over the years. A realist may describe 'moral realism' as 'what you can get away with'; my thanks to Brian Gilmore for the quip.

Chapter Eight: Applying ethics: life and death dilemmas

Fine discussions are in Jonathan Glover, *Causing Death and Saving Lives* (1977). See too Steven Luper, ed., *Life and Death* (2014). The omelette quip is Glover's. Glover is always a good read (see his website). Thomson's violinist 'A Defence of Abortion' is in Peter

Singer, ed., *Applied Ethics* (1986). The little-known Salt comment appears in Singer's *Practical Ethics* (2011).

For commodification: Anne Philips, *Our Bodies, Whose Property* (2013) and Janet Radcliffe Richards, *The Ethics of Transplants* (2012). The former Israeli Prime Minister Ariel Sharon (who died during the writing of this book) had been kept alive, well, his body had, for eight years, despite a persistent vegetative state. Was that the right thing to do – on the grounds of religion, morality, hope against hope – or what?

For enhancing, see Bostrom and Roache, 'Ethical Issues in Human Enhancement' in Ryberg, ed., *New Waves in Applied Ethics* (2007). It is observed: had genetic engineering been present in Victorian times, children might have been designed for piety and patriotism. Rationality, it has been suggested, suggests breeding and engineering should be for moneymakers – as they have better lives in our financially dominated world. R. Jay Wallace's *The View from Here* (2013) illuminates the conflicts in affirming a life that yet rests on conditions meriting regret.

David Hume, in his essay 'On Suicide', draws attention to how people pick and choose regarding when to say we ought not 'to play God'.

Chapter Nine: No man is an island: from community to ecology

G. A. Cohen's appealing, very short, *Why Not Socialism?* (2009) should make us think – see also some Jerry (G. A. Cohen) performances on YouTube – as does the polemical attack on capitalist involvement in poverty, ecological raids *et al.*, in Richard Walker's *Who Cares?* (2011). An inn sign by D. J. Williams – *The Four Alls* (*c.* 1850) – shows one view of society: the King says 'I govern you,' the Bishop, 'I pray for you,' the soldier, 'I fight for you' – and the worker, 'I pay for you.'

For 'forced to be free', see Rousseau's *The Social Contract* (1762). Rousseau was a major influence on the French Revolution and, it seems, not an appealing character; for how the good-humoured David Hume put up with him, see Edmonds and Eidinow, *Rousseau's Dog* (2007).

Many unknown have been at the mercy of oppressive laws where, as E. M. Forster noted and endured, the private individual can suffer from the excessive demands imposed by the norms of the public world. Forster's work as a novelist suffered because, in his day, he had to hide his sexuality from public gaze. Benjamin Britten was nervous of his. Maynard Keynes and others of Cambridge – King's College, Trinity College – and Bloomsbury grew more sanguine.

For structured accessible survey, Jonathan Wolff, *An Introduction to Political Philosophy*, 2nd edn (2006) is excellent. Modern classics are John Rawls, *A Theory of Justice* (1971; revised 1999), no light read, and Robert Nozick, *Anarchy, State and Utopia* (1974). Rawls and Nozick, both of Harvard, put political philosophy back on the map later in the twentieth century. See G. A. Cohen's works for challenges to Nozick. Books by and on Thomas Paine merit delving – for man's rights and how Paine suffered promoting them. Burke is properly assessed in David Bromwich, *The Intellectual Life of Edmund Burke: From the Sublime and Beautiful to American Independence* (2014). Liberty and property – 'the two chief earthly Blessings of human Nature' judged Gilbert Burnet (1643–1715) – have frequently been entwined; eyes are closed to how one person's liberty of property ownership obstructs liberties of others. Behind Rawls's veil, to take another example, one close to the author's London heart and ears – and attempts to think – we may have no view on how noise may affect and distress many people; yet, once in today's cities, we may be baffled as to why laws permit unsilenced drillings, noisy construction works, loud beat music in nearly every bar – and shrill burglar alarms to no purpose.

John Benson, *Environmental Ethics* (2000), is true to its title and includes Paul Taylor's inherent worth and Routley's 'The last man'. Hursthouse (see Chapter Two's notes) includes Tom Regan's animal rights. Moore's 'Two Worlds' is in his *Principia Ethica* (1903); Keynes's description of the ethics, in his *Two Memoirs* (1949).

Salt (1851–1939) appears in Hendrick, *The Savour of Salt* (1989). For past craziness: Edward Payson Evans, *Animal Trials* (2013). Nicholas Humphrey tells of Saxon times when the Welsh village Hawarden allegedly sentenced a Virgin Mary statue because it fell on the Lady of the Castle, killing her (*LRB*, *Letters*, 19.12.2013). The Egyptologist, Petrie, spoke of the deliberate and casual destruction of archaeological remains as an immorality.

Chapter Ten: 'For every foot, its own shoe'

Williams introduced Gauguin; see the Statman collection *Moral Luck* (1993) and R. Jay Wallace, *The View from Here* (2013). Peter Winch's *Ethics and Action* (1972) resists Sidgwick, using Billy Budd; for Iris Murdoch, *The Sovereignty of Good* (1970) and Justin Broackes ed., *Iris Murdoch, Philosopher* (2011) especially for Julia Driver, who also uses Montaigne's 'shoe'. John Wisdom, a twentieth-century jodhpur-wearing Cambridge philosopher, tells of the Taj Mahal in *Paradox and Discovery* (1965).

Sartre introduced the Other in *Being and Nothingness* (mentioned above). For Nietzsche's eternal recurrence: *The Gay Science* (1887) and Michael Tanner's *Nietzsche* (again). Bertrand Russell said he would welcome living his life again – but whether exactly the same, and repeatedly…? Some manage 'yes' to life through lust: according to Percy Grainger, Delius worshipped sex, practising immorality with puritanical stubbornness. Some feel battered by events as in Samuel Beckett's *The End* (trans. Richard Seaver, 1977) – whence the chapter's Beckett quotation.

Personal identity and death *et al.* are in Derek Parfit, *Reasons and Persons* (1984). Samuel Scheffler introduces collective after-living, using P. D. James's story – *The Children of Men* (1992) – in

Death and the After Life (2013). Privacy invasions are in Sophie Bolat, unpublished (2012) MA dissertation, who notes Virginia Woolf's description of private life as 'infinitely the dearest of our possessions'. Forster tells of Goldie in the biography (1934). For more on death, losing oneself and aesthetics, see my *Philosophy: A Beginner's Guide* (2012) and *Humanism* (2009). The Epilogue notes below contain references to some artistic works to try.

Epilogue: 'Buddy, can you spare a dime?'

The title's song, written in the American Great Depression, initially condemned as anti-capitalist, lyrics by Harburg, music by Gorney, was based on a Jewish Russian lullaby. For solidarity and brotherhood, see Wiggins, 'Solidarity and the Root of the Ethical' – and thanks to Zeki Bolat for stimulating some examples.

For reflections on public and personal morality through the colourful life – bohemian yet also establishment – of John Maynard Keynes and his detestation of the love of money, his connections with Moore, Virginia Woolf and the Bloomsbury Group, his urging of social reforms and his questioning of family and business relations, see Backhouse and Bateman, eds, *The Cambridge Companion to Keynes* (2006) – especially papers by Baldwin and Goodwin. Writes Keynes ('The Future'): 'We shall honour those who can teach us how to pluck the hour and the day virtuously and well, the delightful people who are capable of taking direct enjoyment in things, the lilies of the field who toil not, neither do they spin.'

Jesus' words quoted are from Mark (8:36). With deference to tradition and charm, I have used the translation of the 1611 King James Bible.

Walking a mile in another man's shoes provides the safety, of course, of leaving him a mile behind, barefoot – valuable, if you are going to judge him severely. I owe the quip to Ed Winters courtesy of Maltravers.

Life's meaning can no doubt gain some exposure through film, paintings, even popular music and musicals – I bow to others – and certainly mis-meanings through splendid sitcoms such as *Seinfeld* and *Curb*. Schopenhauer emphasized music's deeper value and mystery, found in the classical. I mention below some pieces, often available on YouTube, not as well known as the wonders of Monteverdi, Purcell and J. S. Bach's passions and cantatas, as the achievements of Beethoven, Schubert and Wagner.

For beauteous melancholy, Richard Strauss, *Vier Letzte Lieder (Four Last Songs)* and Mahler, *Ich bin der Welt abhanden gekommen (I am lost to the world)*; ageing and competing passions, Benjamin Britten, *Death in Venice*; mortality's desirability, Janáček, *The Makropulos Case*; political controversy, John Adams, *The Death of Klinghoffer*. Mystery is found in Charles Ives, *The Unanswered Question* and Messiaen, *Quatuor pour la fin du temps (Quartet for the End of Time)*. Musical immersion, with political point – Gandhi and South Africa; Martin Luther King and Civil Rights – is via Philip Glass, *Satyagraha* (note the English National Opera/New York Met production). Life's muddled narratives are present in Berio's *Sinfonia* – note the palimpsest third movement. BBC Radio 3 is the place to go to understand, appreciate and enjoy such music as the above.

For some, possibly less well-known literary endeavours, with characters seeking to comprehend life, try Fallada's novel *Alone in Berlin* (2010); especially Cavafy's poems – Cavafy delightfully described by Forster as 'a Greek gentleman in a straw hat, standing absolutely motionless at a slight angle to the universe' – and Samuel Beckett's plays such as *Rockaby*, *Happy Days* and *Play*.

For an enigmatic ending, since set to music by Steve Reich in *Proverb*, there is Wittgenstein's aphorism:

How small a thought it takes to fill a whole life.

Acknowledgements

Through thousands of years of philosophical discussions – maybe an exaggeration – I am indebted to academic colleagues, friends and numerous students (not mutually exclusive), most recently associated with The Open University and New York University (London) and more distantly with City University London, University College London and King's College, Cambridge. I am also indebted to numerous papers, lectures and conferences, some bright, some baffling, some silly, some all three; they have stimulated, often in forgotten ways. I apologize for the forgetting.

Philosophers and friends who have helped wittingly or unwittingly (in no special order) include Jeremy Barlow, Jonathan Wolff, Malcolm Bishop, Jerry Valberg, Jonathan Katz, Timothy Chappell, Martin Holt, Ray Tallis, Gerard Livingstone, John Shand, Kevin Grant, Peter Atkins, John Cottingham, Alison Fleming, Ben Beaumont, Jesse Tomalty and Michael Clark. Special thanks, for philosophical insight, early read throughs and encouragement, to Sophie Bolat and Derek Matravers.

For additional help, practical and motivational, I thank Oneworld's Mike Harpley, Andrea d'Cruz and Paul Nash.

Because of the astonishing amount of noisy building and road works (possibly I have already alluded to such) in central London, often repetitious and unnecessary – lasers or similar silencing could be developed, together with appreciation of the shabby – I hid away in the relative calm of the Athenaeum's library. I should also mention the pointless, repetitive loud mis-alarms of car and burglar alarms, always ignored (at least in London). I thank, therefore, the ever helpful staff of the club for library and archive support, coffee support and much else, including trips to the London Library, often undertaken by Laura Doran and Annette Rockall in good humour and bad weather.

The Algae, in particular Dan Cohn-Sherbok and Hazhir Teirmourian, often stimulated my thinking, as did other club members – and I thank Angela Joy Harvey for many years of encouragement and philosophical discussion.

My greatest philosophical indebtedness is to Ardon Lyon. If I keep saying this, one day he may feel that he really must get his fine and refined thoughts properly down on paper and published, to put the philosophical world to rights – well, at least pointing in the right direction of clarity and carefulness, not to be confused with ever-growing technical apparatus currently, it seems, in vogue.

♈

While completing this work, Laurence Goldstein died; an 'out of the blue' brain tumour arrived. Laurence devoted his life to philosophy, with splendid humour and fineness of touch – ever helpful, ever thoughtful, ever witty. Laurence was a close philosophical 'buddy' and stimulus; he would spare a dime.

Apparently, when interviewed for membership of an exclusive Hong Kong club, Laurence confessed to being a logician – 'Splendid,' came the reply, 'We could do with a magician.' Well, Laurence could work the magic in many ways; and philosophical reasoning, be its focus logic or ethics, can pull lost rabbits out of hats – and then lose them again.

Index

Where a topic is given major coverage locators are in **bold**.